Wedding RIBBONRY

Ribbon Creations and Decorating Inspirations for the Perfect Wedding

by
Camela Nitschke

Pastimes™

Camela Nitschke
Wedding Ribbonry

Copyright © 2000 by Landauer Corporation

This book was designed and produced by Landauer Books
A division of Landauer Corporation
12251 Maffitt Road, Cumming, Iowa 50061

President and Publisher: Jeramy Lanigan Landauer
Vice President: Becky Johnston
Managing Editor: Marlene Hemberger Heuertz
Art Director: Laurel Albright
Creative Director: Margaret Sindelar
Location Photography Stylist: Mary Anne Thomson
Calligrapher: Cheryl O. Adams
Photographers: Craig Anderson, Amy Cooper, and Dennis Kennedy
Wedding Photographer: Sharon Angel-Beck
Illustrator: Stewart Cott

Published by Martingale & Company
PO Box 118, Bothell, WA 98041-0118 USA

This book is printed on acid-free paper.
Printed in China.

Library of Congress Cataloging-in-Publication Data

Nitschke, Camela, 1948-
    Wedding Ribbonry: ribbon creations and decorating inspirations for the perfect wedding
    by Camela Nitschke.
        p.cm.
    ISBN 1-56477-244-6 (softcover)
        1. Ribbon work. 2. Wedding decorations. I. Title.

TT850.5.N5724 2000
745.594'l--dc21

99-047875

10 9 8 7 6 5 4 3 2 1

CONTENTS

INTRODUCTION

For many years, one of my greatest joys has been creating with ribbons. I can honestly say that it has become a passion for me and will continue to be for as long I as live. With each new research journey to France where intricate silk ribbons were initially created on 17th-century looms, I discover more about the history and heritage of ribbon. I have shared much of my discovery in two previous books, *A Passion for Ribbonry* and *Christmas Ribbonry*.

Anticipating a twilight reception...

So, it was only natural when my daughter, Heather, and her fiancé, Andrew, were planning a romantic summer wedding to include ribbon creations and decorating inspirations for the perfect wedding.

In planning all the wedding details Heather chose a lavender and blue color theme. I began designing with ribbons, including a silver-toned ivory metallic ribbon for a luminescent quality. To make it even more special, I created a Heather rose in honor of the bride!

First I completed the usual bridal accessories, including the headpiece for the veil and the bouquet. The results were so inspirational that we wove ribbons into almost every aspect of the wedding—right down to the delicate flower clusters on the bridesmaids' dresses and the crystal celebration flutes for the bride and groom's toast.

As can be expected, Heather and Andy's wedding was beautiful and it will be a memory her father, Steve, and I shall always treasure. We're already looking forward to future weddings and memories with our other children—Meigen, Maribeth, and Stephen. Since memories are so important, to the final chapter we've added Heather's memory box from the wedding for inspiration. You'll find several easy-to-make keepsakes such as the memory wreath for your special bride and groom to take with them to their new home.

I hope that Heather's memorable wedding and garden reception lavished with exquisite ribbon creations will inspire you to create your own magical wedding memories with ribbon—simple pleasures made by hand, given with love, and shared with all the best wishes for future bliss!

Camela Nitschke

THE BRIDE

Veil

Bouquet

Gloves

Purse

Bible Cover

Veil

❧

Rich with tradition, the veil has been worn by brides throughout the
centuries. It's easy to embellish a purchased bridal headpiece frame with the
bride's favorite flowers, including sweet peas and the Heather rose. Make
each flower individually on a square of buckram. Trim the buckram close to
the stitching before attaching each flower to the headpiece frame. Fill in
with fan flowers, buds, leaves, and ribbon loops. Use a ribbon button center
for the Heather rose and stamens for other roses.

❧

RIBBON FLOWERS

5	Fan Flower	(page 81)
6	Heather Rose	(page 82)
9	Posy (5-Petal)	(page 84)
10	Sweet Pea & Bud	(page 86)
12	Wedding Rose	(page 90)
13	Leaf	(page 92)
14	Ribbon Loops	(page 92)

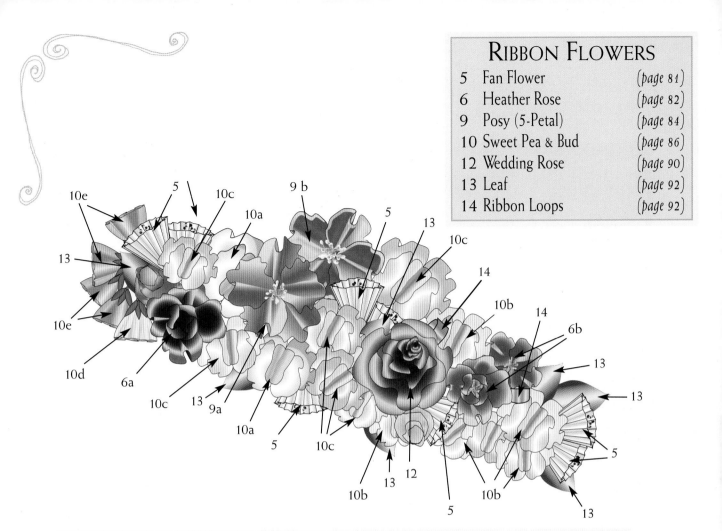

MATERIALS

FABRIC

2" square of buckram for EACH flower

Purchased bridal headpiece frame

RIBBON

(Makes One)

FAN FLOWER

5: 4" of 1"-wide white pleated sheer

HEATHER ROSE

6a: 1 1/2 yards of 1"-wide
light lavender satin

6b: 1 1/2 yards of 1/2"-wide
dark purple grosgrain

POSY (5-PETAL)

9a, b: 1/4 yard of 5/8"-wide light purple
(a) OR dark purple (b) vintage ruffled-
edge OR striped satin-edge taffeta

SWEET PEA

10a, b, c: 3/4 yard of 1"-wide white (a)
OR pale pink (b) OR light pink (c)
shaded taffeta

SWEET PEA BUD

10d, e: 6" of 1"-wide pale pink (d)
OR light pink (e) shaded taffeta

WEDDING ROSE

12: 1 yard of 1"-wide medium lavender
striped satin-edge taffeta

LEAF

13: 5" of 5/8"-wide
light green wire-edge taffeta

RIBBON LOOPS

14: 3" of 3/8"-wide medium
green satin-edge pleated rayon

Bouquet

The bridal bouquet will become a treasured heirloom when the flowers are made of ribbon. Numerous cabochon roses make it easy to quickly fill a purchased bouquet form with everlasting blooms. Make each flower individually on a square of buckram. Trim the buckram close to the stitching before attaching each flower. Create a stem for each from cotton-wrapped floral wire. Arrange as desired on the bouquet form. Add leaves, buds, purchased stamens, and wired pearl clusters.

For finishing, add a ruffling of sheer contrast ribbon and a bow with knotted ribbon streamers.

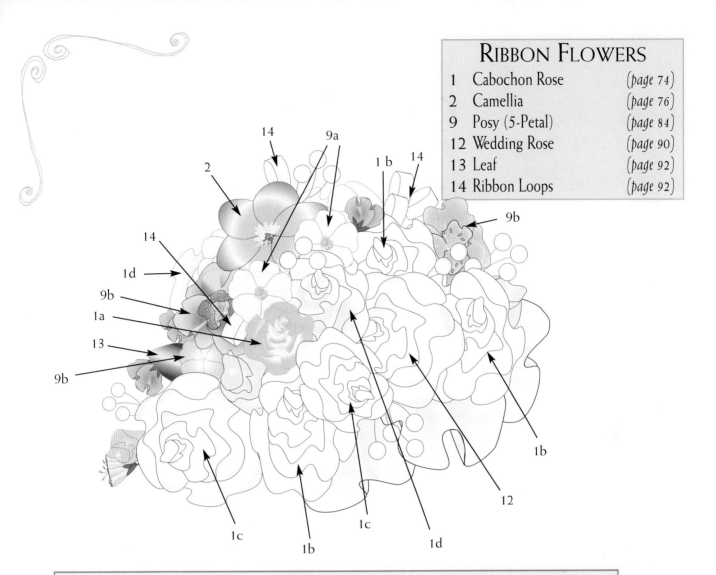

MATERIALS

FABRIC

2" square of buckram for EACH flower

Purchased bouquet form with handle

RIBBON

(Makes One)

CABOCHON ROSE

1a: 1 yard of 1"-wide
medium blue taffeta

1b, c, d: 1 yard of 1 1/2"-wide ivory (b)
OR white (c) OR light pink (d) taffeta OR
satin-edge moiré taffeta OR satin/sheer

CAMELLIA

2: 1 1/2 yards of 1 1/2"-wide
light purple bias-cut silk

POSY (5-PETAL)

9a: 1/4 yard of 1/2"-wide gold
sheer metallic

9b: 1/3 yard of 1"-wide
light lavender picot-edge sheer

WEDDING ROSE

12: 1 yard of 1 1/2"-wide
white sheer

LEAF

13: 5" of 1/2"-wide
medium green iridescent taffeta

RIBBON LOOPS

14: 3" of 3/8"-wide silver
satin-edge pleated rayon

Gloves

A bouquet of cabochon roses in miniature trims each glove. Make each flower individually on a square of buckram. Trim the buckram close to the stitching. Arrange the completed cabochon roses in groups of five on the felt circle.

For finishing, add a ruffling of sheer contrast ribbon with multi-loops to each miniature bouquet and attach securely to the glove at the wrist.

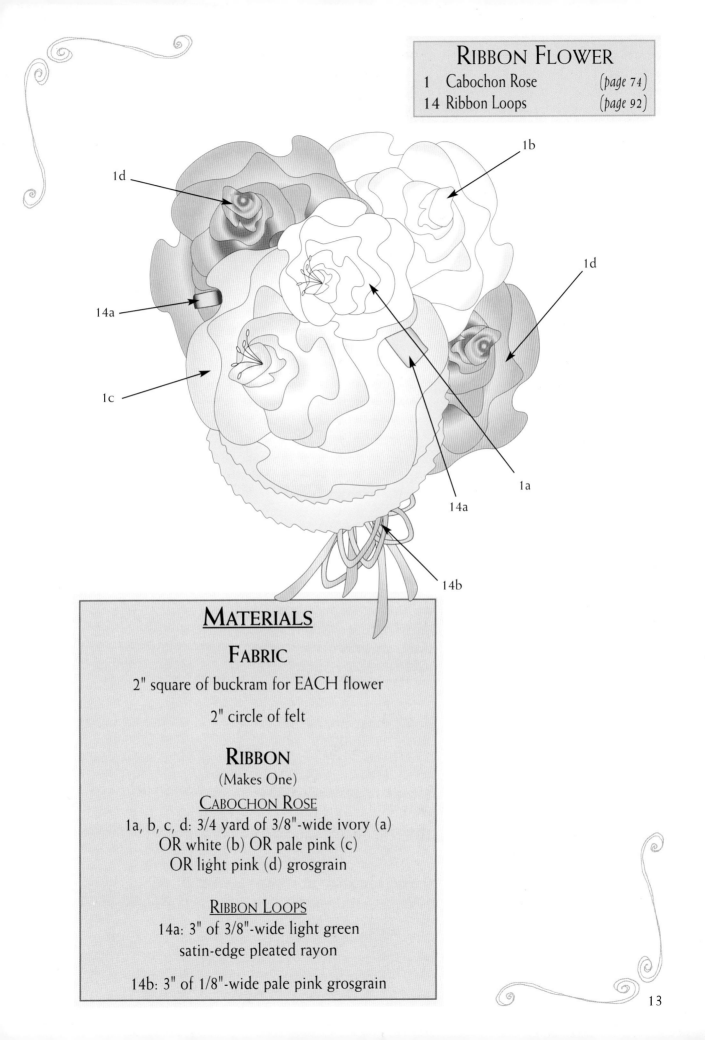

1d

1b

1d

14a

1c

1a

14a

14b

MATERIALS

FABRIC

2" square of buckram for EACH flower

2" circle of felt

RIBBON

(Makes One)

CABOCHON ROSE

1a, b, c, d: 3/4 yard of 3/8"-wide ivory (a)
OR white (b) OR pale pink (c)
OR light pink (d) grosgrain

RIBBON LOOPS

14a: 3" of 3/8"-wide light green
satin-edge pleated rayon

14b: 3" of 1/8"-wide pale pink grosgrain

Purse

For the bride's purse, use a favorite evening bag pattern or purchase an evening bag. Make each flower individually on a square of buckram. Trim the buckram close to the stitching before attaching each flower to the circle of felt. Attach the circle with flowers to the front flap as shown above.

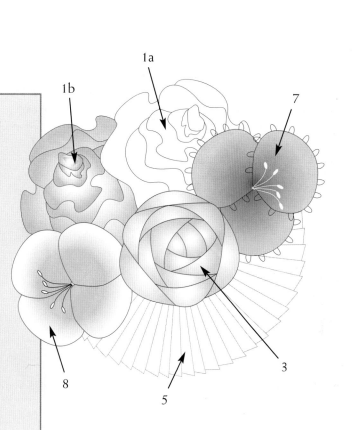

MATERIALS

FABRIC

2" square of buckram
for EACH flower

2 1/2" circle of felt

RIBBON
(Makes One)

CABOCHON ROSE

1a: 1/2 yard of 5/8"-wide
white satin/sheer

1b: 1/2 yard of 5/8"-wide
medium lavender taffeta

CHOU ROSE
3: 1/2 yard of 5/8"-wide
light purple satin

FAN FLOWER
5: 4" of 1"-wide
white pleated satin

POSY (3-PETAL)
7: 7" of 3/4"-wide light blue
picot-edge sheer

POSY (4-PETAL)
8: 7" of 5/8"-wide
light purple shaded rayon

RIBBON FLOWERS

1	Cabochon Rose	(page 74)
3	Chou Rose	(page 78)
5	Fan Flower	(page 81)
7	Posy (3-Petal)	(page 84)
8	Posy (4-Petal)	(page 84)

Bible Cover

For the ceremony, accent the bride's Bible cover with petite ribbon sweet peas to coordinate with her bouquet and gloves. Make each flower individually using a variety of color combinations on a square of buckram. Trim the buckram close to the stitching before attaching each flower. Arrange completed flowers on the felt circle and attach securely to the front of the Bible cover (ours is 4" x 6"). Glue ribbon loops, ribbon tails, and soutache braid stems in place. Fold leaf in half and whipstitch edges together; glue in place.

For finishing, add knotted ribbon streamers for a bookmark as desired.

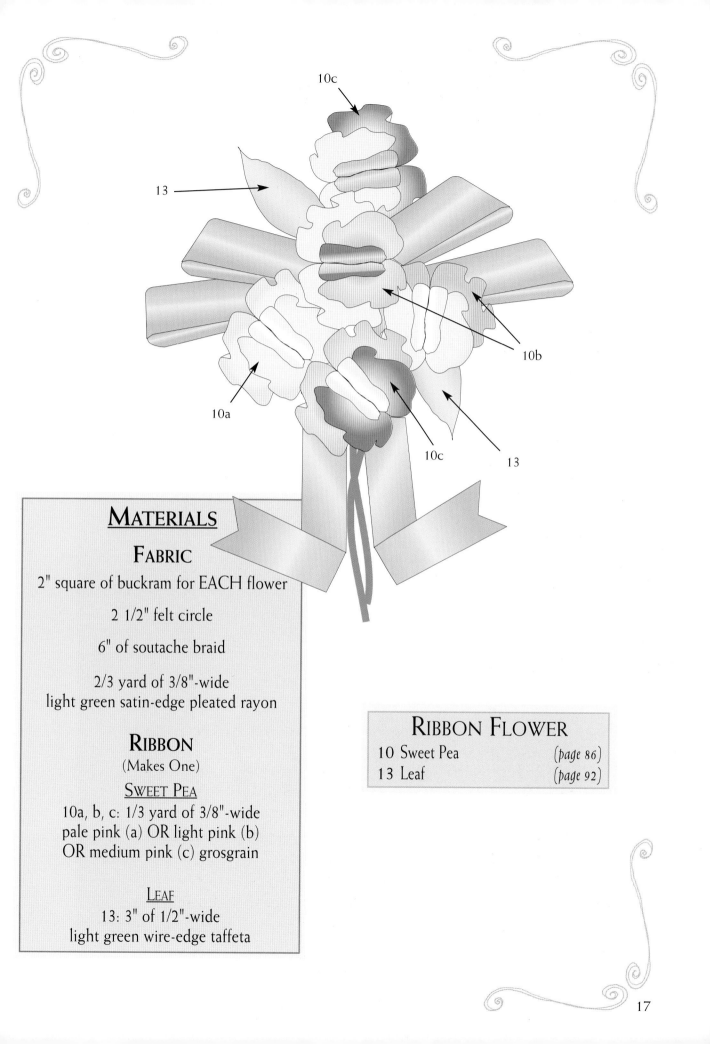

MATERIALS

FABRIC

2" square of buckram for EACH flower

2 1/2" felt circle

6" of soutache braid

2/3 yard of 3/8"-wide
light green satin-edge pleated rayon

RIBBON
(Makes One)

SWEET PEA
10a, b, c: 1/3 yard of 3/8"-wide
pale pink (a) OR light pink (b)
OR medium pink (c) grosgrain

LEAF
13: 3" of 1/2"-wide
light green wire-edge taffeta

RIBBON FLOWER

10 Sweet Pea	(page 86)
13 Leaf	(page 92)

THE WEDDING PARTY

Mother of the Bride's Hat

Junior Bridesmaid's Dress Trims

Bridesmaid's Shoulder Cascade

Flower Girl's Head Wreath

Flower Girl's Basket

Rings Pillow

Mother of the Groom's Hat

Mother of the Bride's Hat

A special hat trimmed just for the mother of the bride is always in style. A sheer white brimmed hat like the one shown here provides the perfect background for a cluster of her favorite flowers. Make each flower individually on a square of buckram. Trim the buckram close to the stitching before attaching each flower to the ribbon-banded hat.

Complete the arrangement by interspersing a variety of small and large leaves among the flowers.

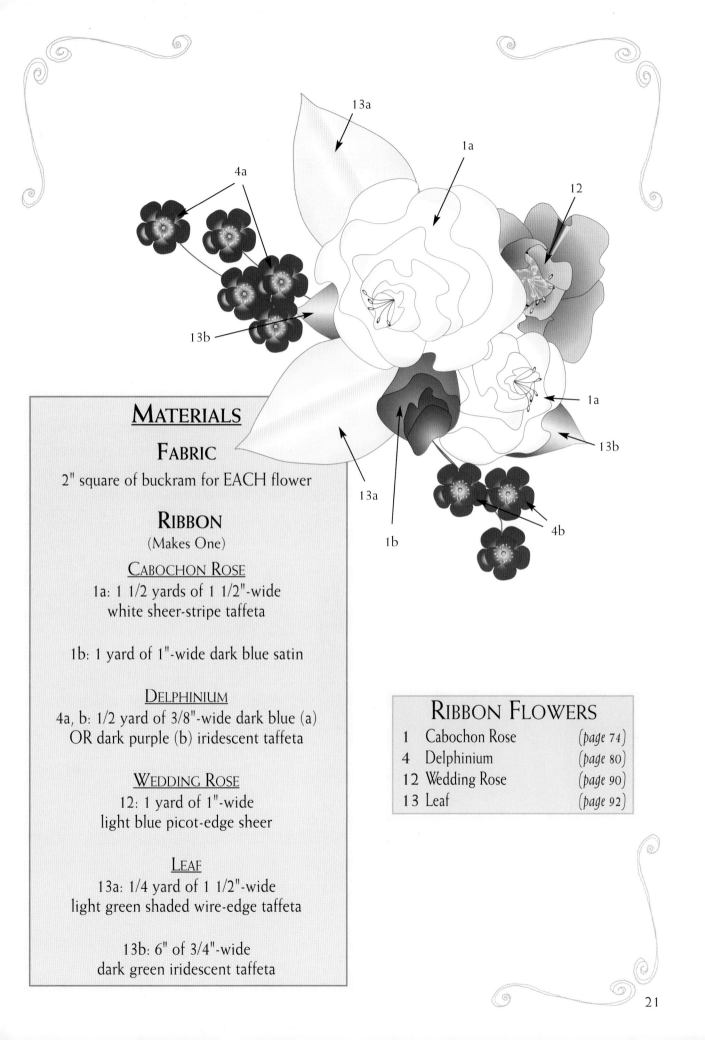

13a

1a

12

4a

13b

1a

13b

13a

1b

4b

MATERIALS

FABRIC

2" square of buckram for EACH flower

RIBBON

(Makes One)

CABOCHON ROSE

1a: 1 1/2 yards of 1 1/2"-wide
white sheer-stripe taffeta

1b: 1 yard of 1"-wide dark blue satin

DELPHINIUM

4a, b: 1/2 yard of 3/8"-wide dark blue (a)
OR dark purple (b) iridescent taffeta

WEDDING ROSE

12: 1 yard of 1"-wide
light blue picot-edge sheer

LEAF

13a: 1/4 yard of 1 1/2"-wide
light green shaded wire-edge taffeta

13b: 6" of 3/4"-wide
dark green iridescent taffeta

RIBBON FLOWERS

1	Cabochon Rose	(page 74)
4	Delphinium	(page 80)
12	Wedding Rose	(page 90)
13	Leaf	(page 92)

Junior Bridesmaid's Dress Trims

The junior bridesmaid's dress takes on a custom look with an underskirt of white bridal satin trimmed with a floral scattering of sweet miniatures and covered by pale lavender organdy with a shirred scalloped hemline.

Make each flower individually on a square of buckram. (Centers of flowers can be stamens or seed beads.) Trim the buckram close to the stitching before attaching each flower to form a cluster on the felt circle.

Add buds, leaves, and loops as desired. For finishing, add a sash and bow of layered organdy and satin.

Choose a favorite flower cluster to display on the dress bodice for a final accent.

MATERIALS

FABRIC

2" square of buckram for EACH flower

2" circle of felt for each cluster

RIBBON

(Makes One)

FAN FLOWER

5a, b: 4" of 1/2"-wide medium lavender (a) OR dark lavender (b) pleated satin

5c: 4" of 7/8"-wide light lavender pleated sheer

POSY (4-PETAL)

8a: 7" of 5/8"-wide light purple taffeta

8b: 7" of 1"-wide gold metallic sheer

POSY (5-PETAL)

9a: 9" of 5/8"-wide light purple taffeta

9b: 9" of 3/8"-wide silver metallic sheer

9c: 9" of 1/2"-wide light purple grosgrain

9d: 9" of 5/8"-wide dark lavender satin

VIOLA

11a, b: 1/4 yard of 5/8"-wide medium blue (a) AND 5" of 5/8"-wide light purple (b) satin

LEAF

13: 5" of 5/8"-wide dark green wire-edge taffeta

RIBBON LOOPS

14a: 3" of 3/8"-wide medium green satin-edge pleated rayon

14b: 3" of 1/8"-wide medium green grosgrain

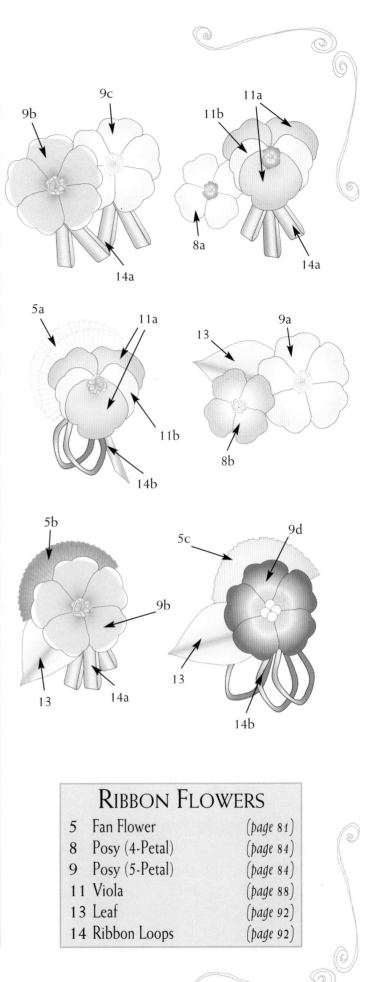

RIBBON FLOWERS

5	Fan Flower	(page 81)
8	Posy (4-Petal)	(page 84)
9	Posy (5-Petal)	(page 84)
11	Viola	(page 88)
13	Leaf	(page 92)
14	Ribbon Loops	(page 92)

Bridesmaid's Shoulder Cascade

❧

Reviving a Victorian tradition, the shoulder cascade is a charming accent for the bridesmaid's dress or any pretty summer gown. Select as many flowers from the chart, opposite, as desired. Make each flower individually on a square of buckram. Trim the buckram close to the stitching before attaching each flower. Arrange flowers as shown in your own artful floral cascade on the 8"-square buckram foundation. Add the leaves and stamens to the flower centers as desired, and trim with one or two M bows in the bride's colors.

If desired, for finishing cover buckram with felt and attach purchased pin back.

❧

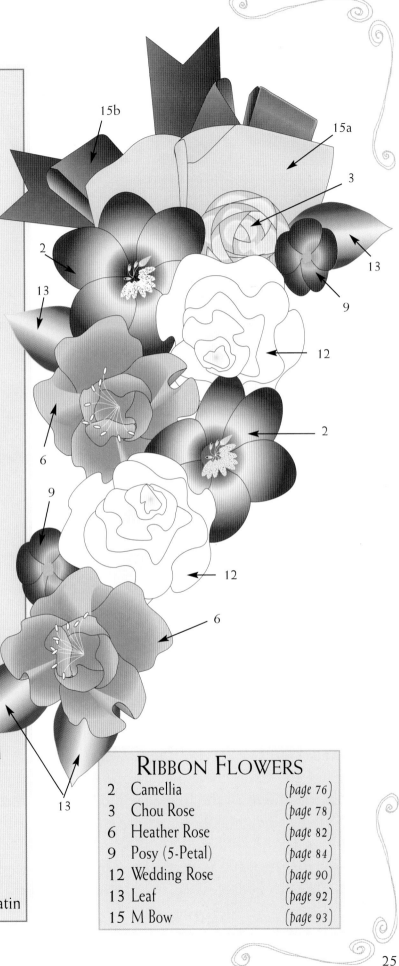

MATERIALS

FABRIC

2" square of buckram
for EACH flower

8" square of buckram

RIBBON
(Makes One)

CAMELLIA
2: 1 1/2 yards of 1 1/2"-wide
medium blue bias-cut silk

CHOU ROSE
3: 3/4 yard of 1"-wide
light purple satin

HEATHER ROSE
6: 1 1/2 yards of 1"-wide
light blue picot-edge sheer

POSY (5-PETAL)
9: 9" of 3/4"-wide
dark blue satin

WEDDING ROSE
12: 1 yard of 1"-wide
silver metallic sheer

LEAF
13: 7" of 1/2"-wide medium green
wire-edge taffeta

M BOW
15a: 3/4 yard of 2"-wide
light blue metallic sheer

15b: 3/4 yard of 1"-wide dark blue satin

RIBBON FLOWERS

2	Camellia	(page 76)
3	Chou Rose	(page 78)
6	Heather Rose	(page 82)
9	Posy (5-Petal)	(page 84)
12	Wedding Rose	(page 90)
13	Leaf	(page 92)
15	M Bow	(page 93)

Flower Girl's Head Wreath

⟨∾⟩

Reminiscent of yesteryear, the flower girl is wreathed in a crown of flowers. To make the simple head wreath shown here, measure the child's head and adjust the length of the foundation circle of covered belting accordingly. Make each flower individually on a square of buckram. Trim the buckram close to the stitching before attaching the flowers according to the illustration, opposite. Repeat the sequence as needed to cover the circumference of the head wreath, filling in with buds, leaves, and loops as desired.

⟨∾⟩

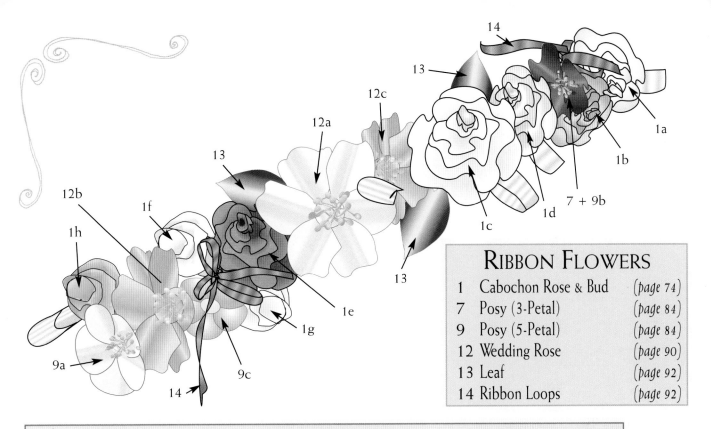

Materials

Fabric

2" square of buckram for EACH flower

24" piece of 3/4"-wide belting covered with fabric of choice

Ribbon
(Makes One)

Cabochon Rose

1a: 1 yard of 1"-wide
white sheer/satin stripe

1b: 1 yard of 1"-wide medium
lavender pleated taffeta

1c: 1 yard of 1"-wide
gold satin-edge sheer

1d, e: 1 yard of 5/8"-wide pale
pink (d) OR medium pink (e) taffeta

Cabochon Rose Bud

1f: 6" of 1"-wide white
sheer/satin stripe

1g: 6" of 1"-wide gold
satin-edge sheer

1h: 6" of 5/8"-wide medium pink taffeta

Posy (3-Petal)

7: 9" of 1/2"-wide dark blue shaded taffeta

Posy (5-Petal)

9a, b, c: 9" of 1/2"-wide
white (a) OR dark blue (b) OR
light purple (c) shaded taffeta

Wedding Rose

12a, b, c: 1 yard of 1"-wide white (a)
OR medium pink (b) OR
light purple (c) pleated satin-edge sheer

Leaf

13: 4" of 5/8"-wide medium
green wire-edge taffeta

Ribbon Loops:

14a: 3" of 3/8"-wide light green
satin-edge pleated rayon

14b: 3" of 1/8"-wide
medium green grosgrain

Flower Girl's Basket

The flower girl's basket can be as simple or elaborate as the wedding itself. Here, the plain wicker basket and handle are wrapped with elegant sculptured bridal satin. Make each flower individually on a square of buckram. Trim the buckram close to the stitching before attaching the flowers to the buckram foundation. Fill in with buds and leaves as desired. Nestle the completed arrangement onto a double M bow to match the bride's colors.

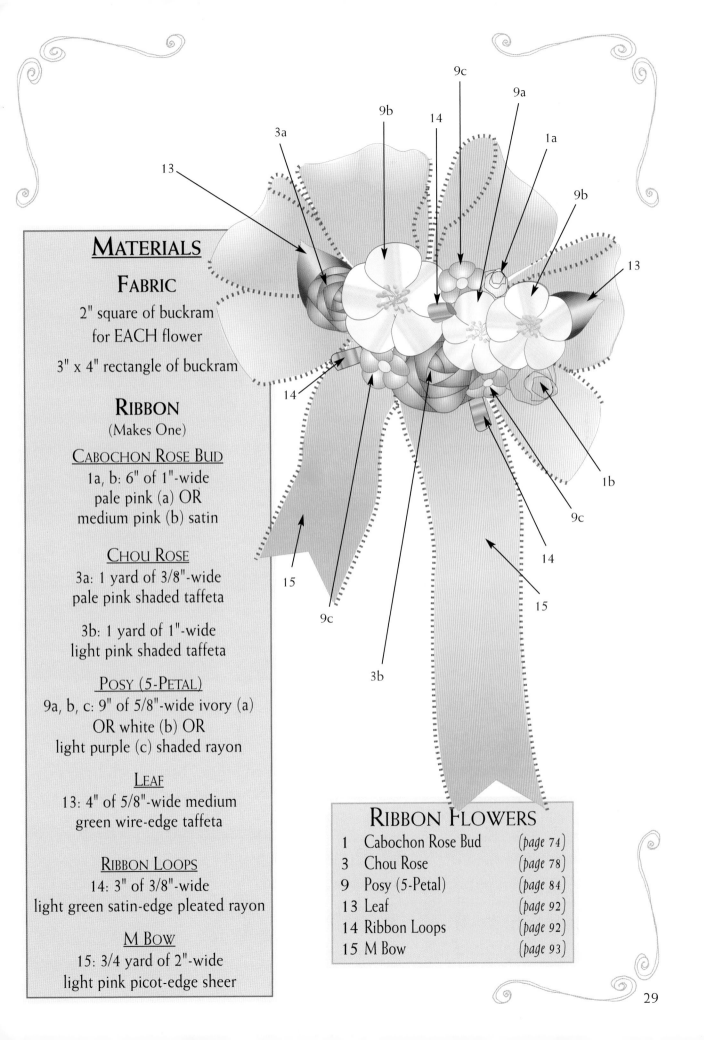

MATERIALS

FABRIC

2" square of buckram
for EACH flower

3" x 4" rectangle of buckram

RIBBON
(Makes One)

CABOCHON ROSE BUD
1a, b: 6" of 1"-wide
pale pink (a) OR
medium pink (b) satin

CHOU ROSE
3a: 1 yard of 3/8"-wide
pale pink shaded taffeta

3b: 1 yard of 1"-wide
light pink shaded taffeta

POSY (5-PETAL)
9a, b, c: 9" of 5/8"-wide ivory (a)
OR white (b) OR
light purple (c) shaded rayon

LEAF
13: 4" of 5/8"-wide medium
green wire-edge taffeta

RIBBON LOOPS
14: 3" of 3/8"-wide
light green satin-edge pleated rayon

M BOW
15: 3/4 yard of 2"-wide
light pink picot-edge sheer

RIBBON FLOWERS

1	Cabochon Rose Bud	(page 74)
3	Chou Rose	(page 78)
9	Posy (5-Petal)	(page 84)
13	Leaf	(page 92)
14	Ribbon Loops	(page 92)
15	M Bow	(page 93)

Rings Pillow

To enhance the ring ceremony, start with a purchased pillow. Make each flower individually on a square of buckram. Trim the buckram close to the stitching before attaching flowers to the 4" buckram foundation. The completed flowers will form a cluster. Sew it onto an M bow along with a generous length of 1/4"-wide coordinating satin ribbon for each ring and half a dozen multicolored ribbons knotted at intervals. Attach the M bow with flowers and ribbons to the center of the pillow, anchoring it securely.

Tie the bride and groom's rings just below the cluster.

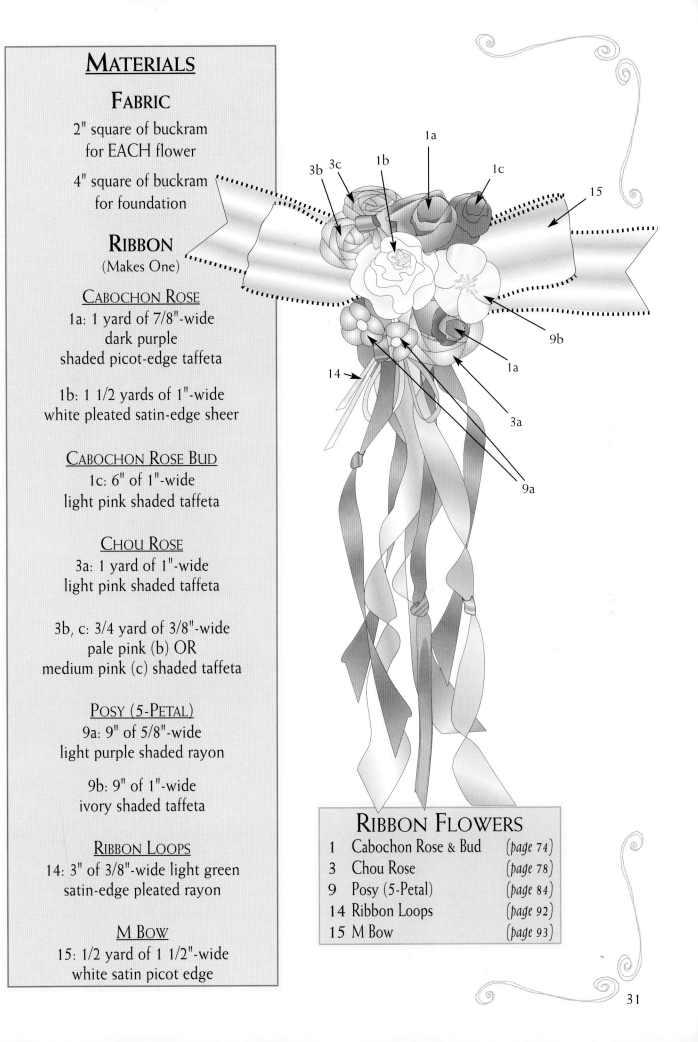

MATERIALS

FABRIC

2" square of buckram
for EACH flower

4" square of buckram
for foundation

RIBBON
(Makes One)

CABOCHON ROSE
1a: 1 yard of 7/8"-wide
dark purple
shaded picot-edge taffeta

1b: 1 1/2 yards of 1"-wide
white pleated satin-edge sheer

CABOCHON ROSE BUD
1c: 6" of 1"-wide
light pink shaded taffeta

CHOU ROSE
3a: 1 yard of 1"-wide
light pink shaded taffeta

3b, c: 3/4 yard of 3/8"-wide
pale pink (b) OR
medium pink (c) shaded taffeta

POSY (5-PETAL)
9a: 9" of 5/8"-wide
light purple shaded rayon

9b: 9" of 1"-wide
ivory shaded taffeta

RIBBON LOOPS
14: 3" of 3/8"-wide light green
satin-edge pleated rayon

M BOW
15: 1/2 yard of 1 1/2"-wide
white satin picot edge

RIBBON FLOWERS

1	Cabochon Rose & Bud	(page 74)
3	Chou Rose	(page 78)
9	Posy (5-Petal)	(page 84)
14	Ribbon Loops	(page 92)
15	M Bow	(page 93)

Mother of the Groom's Hat

~

Summer's straw hat is transformed into a stunning accessory for the mother of the groom with a floral medallion featured on a lace-edged satin ribbon tied in a bow. Make each flower individually on a square of buckram. Trim the buckram close to the stitching before attaching the flowers to the 4" circle of buckram, creating a medallion of cabochon roses in shades of pink and white.

For finishing, wrap a wide lace-edged satin ribbon around the hat brim, tie into a bow, and attach the medallion to the center of the bow.

~

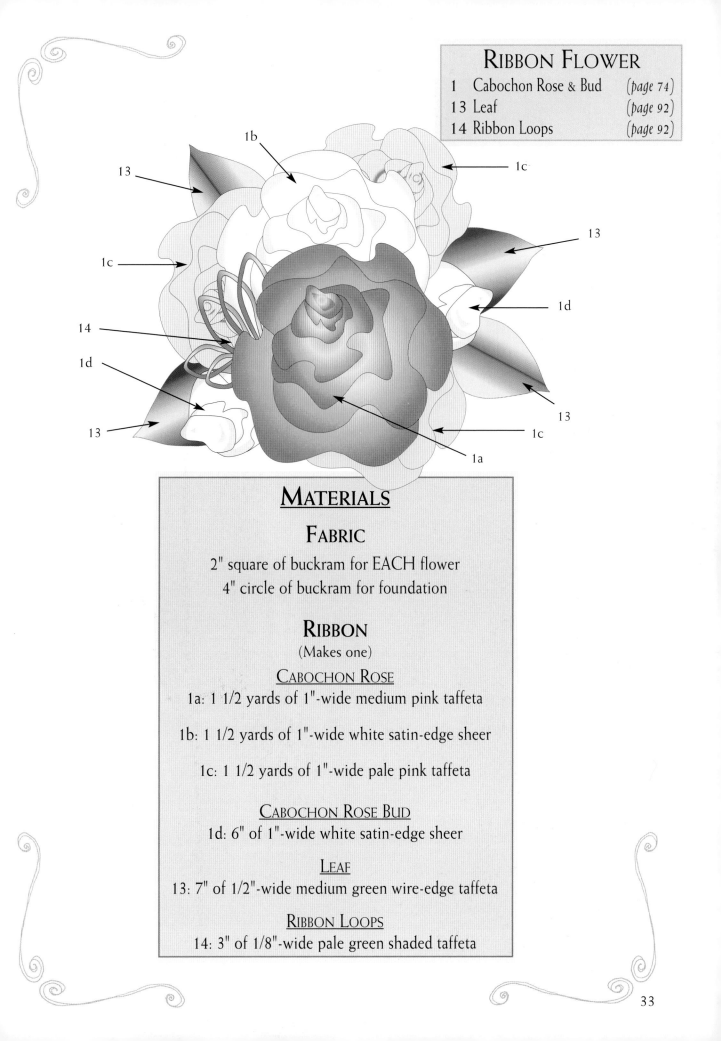

MATERIALS

FABRIC

2" square of buckram for EACH flower
4" circle of buckram for foundation

RIBBON
(Makes one)

CABOCHON ROSE

1a: 1 1/2 yards of 1"-wide medium pink taffeta

1b: 1 1/2 yards of 1"-wide white satin-edge sheer

1c: 1 1/2 yards of 1"-wide pale pink taffeta

CABOCHON ROSE BUD

1d: 6" of 1"-wide white satin-edge sheer

LEAF

13: 7" of 1/2"-wide medium green wire-edge taffeta

RIBBON LOOPS

14: 3" of 1/8"-wide pale green shaded taffeta

THE CEREMONY

Aisle Lantern

Seating Bows

Unity Candle

Aisle Lantern

For a special evening wedding, decorated aisle lanterns provide a romantic glow.

Create loops using wire-edged ribbon of assorted widths. With glue, secure each loop to the lantern pole around the base of the globe. Finish by wrapping with a large satin-edge sheer bow.

Make each flower individually on a square of buckram. Trim the buckram close to the stitching before attaching a cabochon rose or posy to the center front of each loop. Intersperse knotted ribbon streamers as desired.

NOTE: Fill base of globe with cabochon roses ONLY if you plan to cover them completely with a glass or plastic candle drip guard.

1b

1c

1a

8a

8b

MATERIALS

FABRIC

2" square of buckram
for EACH flower

RIBBON

(Makes One)

CABOCHON ROSE
1a: 1 yard of 1"-wide
light purple satin

1b: 2/3 yard of 1"-wide dark blue
iridescent taffeta

1c: 2/3 yard of 1"-wide
medium lavender shaded satin

POSY (4-PETAL)
8a, b: 8" of 5/8"-wide
medium lavender (a) OR
light purple (b) shaded taffeta

RIBBON FLOWERS

1	Cabochon Rose	(page 74)
8	Posy (4-Petal)	(page 84)

Seating Bows

Give special recognition with reserved seating bows for the immediate family members. Start with a purchased wire and moss foundation with floral accents (see Sources & Supplies, page 95) or ask your florist to create one. Make each flower individually on a square of buckram. Trim the buckram close to the stitching before attaching each flower to the moss. Mix ribbon flowers with dried or fresh flowers. Add iridescent sheer ribbon bows as desired.

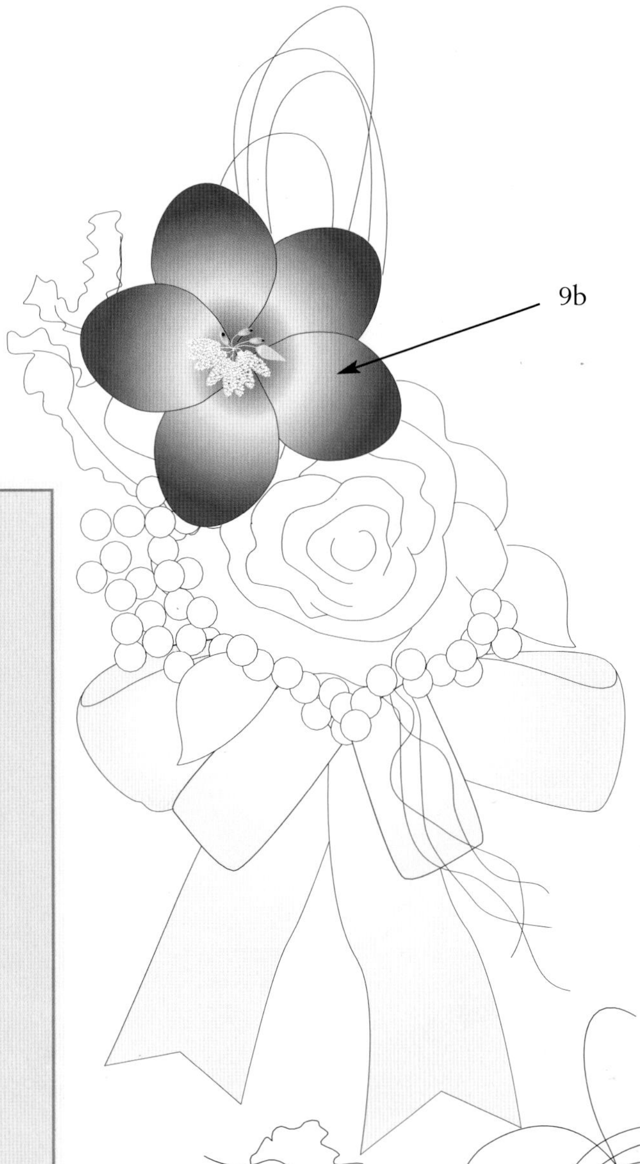

9b

MATERIALS

FABRIC
2" square of buckram
for EACH flower

RIBBON
(Makes One)

<u>POSY (5-PETAL)</u>
9a: 16" of 1"-wide
ivory wire-edge taffeta

9b: 16" of 1 1/2"-wide
dark purple bias-cut silk

<u>VIOLA</u>
11: 14" of 1"-wide
light pink
wire-edge iridescent taffeta

RIBBON FLOWERS

9 Posy (5-Petal)   (page 84)
11 Viola   (page 88)

11

9a

Unity Candle

Surround the unity candle with cabochon ribbon roses mixed with fresh roses, and see whether guests can tell them apart! Make each flower individually on a square of buckram. Trim the buckram close to the stitching. Mix the completed ribbon roses with baby's breath and fresh delphinium blooms. Add a band of 4"-wide vintage Jacquard ribbon to the center of the unity candle.

Trim individual candles with picot-edge ribbon in coordinating colors and tuck a tiny delphinium bloom into each bow.

RIBBON FLOWERS
1 Cabochon Rose *(page 74)*

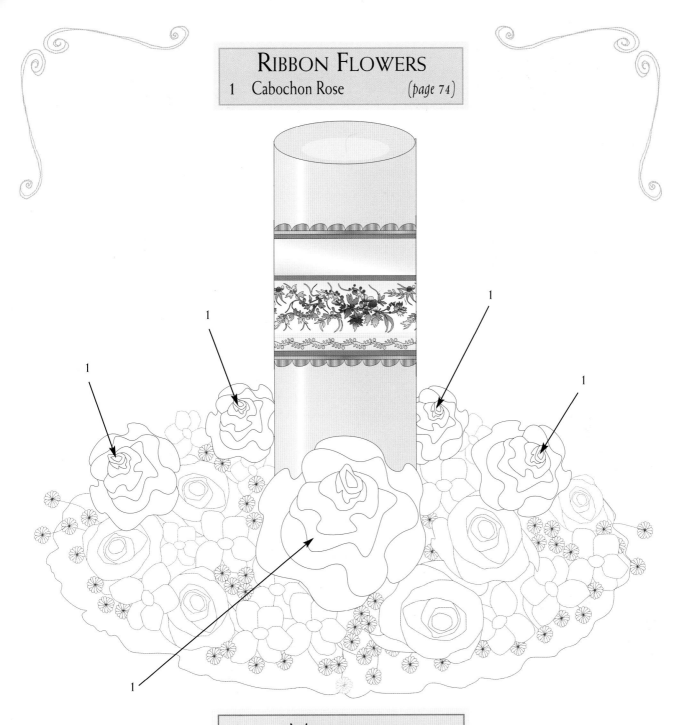

MATERIALS

FABRIC
2" square of buckram
for EACH flower

RIBBON
(Makes One)

<u>CABOCHON ROSE</u>
1: 1 1/2 yards of 1 1/2"-wide
white rayon

THE RECEPTION

Gift Basket

Celebration Flutes

Guest Book

Gift Basket

✑

Welcome your wedding guests to the reception with an exquisite ribbon-trimmed basket for gifts and greetings.

    Line a purchased basket with scallops of heritage lace and trim with a satin bow in the bride's colors. Make each flower individually on a square of buckram. Trim the buckram close to the stitching before attaching each flower to the center of the satin bow. For detail, add stamens to the centers of the flowers.

✑

RIBBON FLOWERS

| 1 | Cabochon Rose | *(page 74)* |
| 9 | Posy (5-Petal) | *(page 84)* |

MATERIALS

FABRIC

2" square of buckram for EACH flower

RIBBON

(Makes One)

CABOCHON ROSE

1: 1 1/2 yards of 1 1/2"-wide
medium lavender taffeta

POSY (5-PETAL)

9: 9" of 1"-wide
white pleated satin-edge sheer

Celebration Flutes

The bride and groom's toast at the wedding reception will be even more memorable with celebration flutes to use again and again for many anniversaries to come! Each glass stem is uniquely embellished with tiny ribbon flowers. Make each flower individually on a square of buckram. Add stamens to the flower centers and complete with assorted leaves and loops. Trim the buckram close to the stitching before attaching each flower to the crystal glass stem with floral wire. Remove flowers before washing stemware.

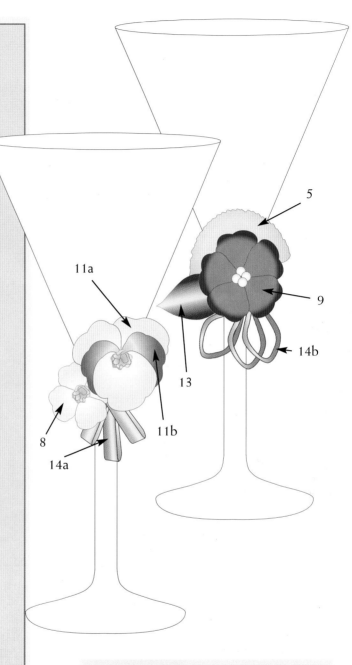

MATERIALS

FABRIC

2" square of buckram
for EACH flower

RIBBON
(Makes One)

FAN FLOWER
5: 4" of 1"-wide
light lavender
ruffled-edge sheer

POSY (4-PETAL)
8: 8" of 1/2"-wide
light purple satin

POSY (5-PETAL)
9: 9" of 1"-wide dark lavender
iridescent taffeta

VIOLA
11a, b: 1/4 yard of 5/8"-wide
light purple (a) AND

5" of 5/8"-wide
dark purple (b) satin

LEAF
13: 5″ of 5/8"-wide
dark green wire-edge taffeta

RIBBON LOOPS
14a: 3" of 3/8"-wide medium green
satin-edge pleated rayon

14b: 3" of 1/8"-wide
medium green grosgrain

RIBBON FLOWERS

5	Fan Flower	(page 81)
8	Posy (4-Petal)	(page 84)
9	Posy (5-Petal)	(page 84)
11	Viola	(page 88)
13	Leaf	(page 92)
14	Ribbon Loops	(page 92)

Guest Book

Invite your guests to register their wedding attendance in style. Trim the guest book with ribbon flowers and heirloom ribbon to match. Make each flower individually on a square of buckram. Trim the buckram close to the stitching before attaching each flower to the center of the 3" circle of buckram. Fill in with several soft, picot-edge sheer ribbon loops and pleated leaves as desired. Attach the buckram foundation to the cover of the guest book (ours is 7 1/2" x 9") and trim with a border of antique ribbon. For a special accent, include a Venetian glass ink pen on a crystal pen rest and a crystal inkwell filled with rose-scented ink!

MATERIALS

FABRIC

2" square buckram for EACH flower

3" circle of buckram

RIBBON
(Makes One)

CABOCHON ROSE BUD
1a: 6" of 1"-wide
ivory striped-satin/taffeta

1b: 6" of 1"-wide
dark purple picot-edge sheer

CHOU ROSE
3: 1/4 yard of 1/2"-wide
light lavender rayon

POSY (4-PETAL)
8: 8" of 1"-wide
dark purple picot-edge sheer

POSY (5-PETAL)
9a: 9" of 1/2"-wide light purple satin

9b: 6" of 1"-wide
ivory striped-satin taffeta

LEAF
13: 4" of 3/8"-wide medium green
satin-edge pleated rayon

RIBBON FLOWERS

1	Cabochon Rose Bud	(page 74)
3	Chou Rose	(page 78)
8	Posy (4-Petal)	(page 84)
9	Posy (5-Petal)	(page 84)
13	Leaf	(page 92)

THE GIFTS

Towel Trims

Pillowcase Embellishments

Basket Sachet

Padded Hanger

Lampshade

Towel Trims

❧

Personalize purchased towels for the bride and groom's new home with a simple band of ribbons top-stitched several inches from the lower edge and a cluster of three-petal posies. Make each flower individually on a square of buckram. (Centers of flowers can be either ruched grosgrain or stamens.) Trim the buckram close to the stitching before attaching each flower to a 2" circle of felt. Add a purchased pin back for easy removal for laundering.

❧

RIBBON FLOWER

| 7 | Posy (3-Petal) | *(page 84)* |
| 14 | Ribbon Loops | *(page 92)* |

7b

7a

14

7a

MATERIALS

FABRIC

2" square of buckram
for EACH flower

2" circle of felt

RIBBON
(Makes One)

POSY (3-PETAL)
7a, b: 7" of 3/8"-wide
white (a) OR
light purple (b) grosgrain

RIBBON LOOPS
14: 3" of 1/4"-wide
medium lavender
shaded grosgrain

Pillowcase Embellishments

Customize a pair of lace-edged pillowcases with an artful combination of varying widths of grosgrain and Jacquard ribbons for a memorable gift for the bride and groom. Start by top-stitching the Jacquard ribbon just above the lace edge of the pillowcase. Position the grosgrain ribbon above the Jacquard ribbon and top-stitch. To make the gift even more special, purchase cotton sateen sheets in coordinating colors and tie with a satin ribbon to match.

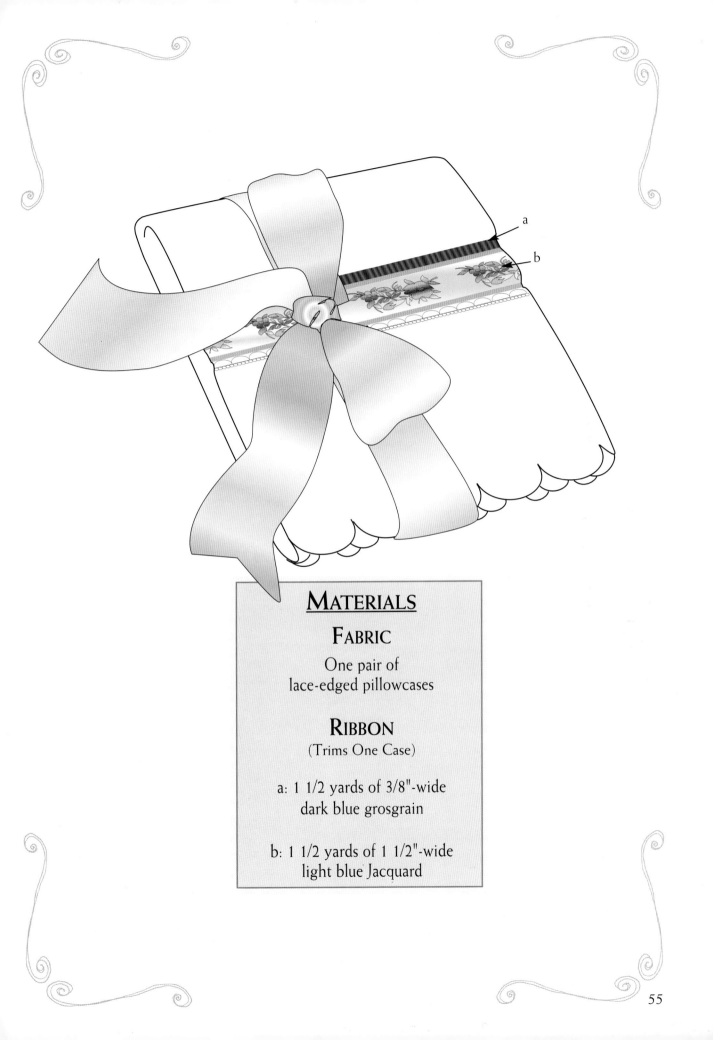

a

b

MATERIALS

FABRIC

One pair of
lace-edged pillowcases

RIBBON

(Trims One Case)

a: 1 1/2 yards of 3/8"-wide
dark blue grosgrain

b: 1 1/2 yards of 1 1/2"-wide
light blue Jacquard

Basket Sachet

Scented sachets are an extra-special gift when you make them in multiples from scraps of heirloom ribbon to match the bride and groom's towels and linens. Make the sachet shown here with ribbon weaving or other fabric. Using the basket-shaped pattern provided, opposite, cut out the two pieces (be sure to add seam allowances). Place them right sides facing and sew around the edges, leaving an opening for turning. When the basket is completed, trim the top with lace and fill it with fragrant potpourri before sewing the top opening closed.

Make each flower individually on a square of buckram. (Centers of flowers can be either ruched grosgrain or stamens.) Trim the buckram close to the stitching before attaching a single delphinium to a tiny satin bow at the basket top. For finishing, add a satin cord for hanging.

RIBBON FLOWER

4   Delphinium   *(page 80)*

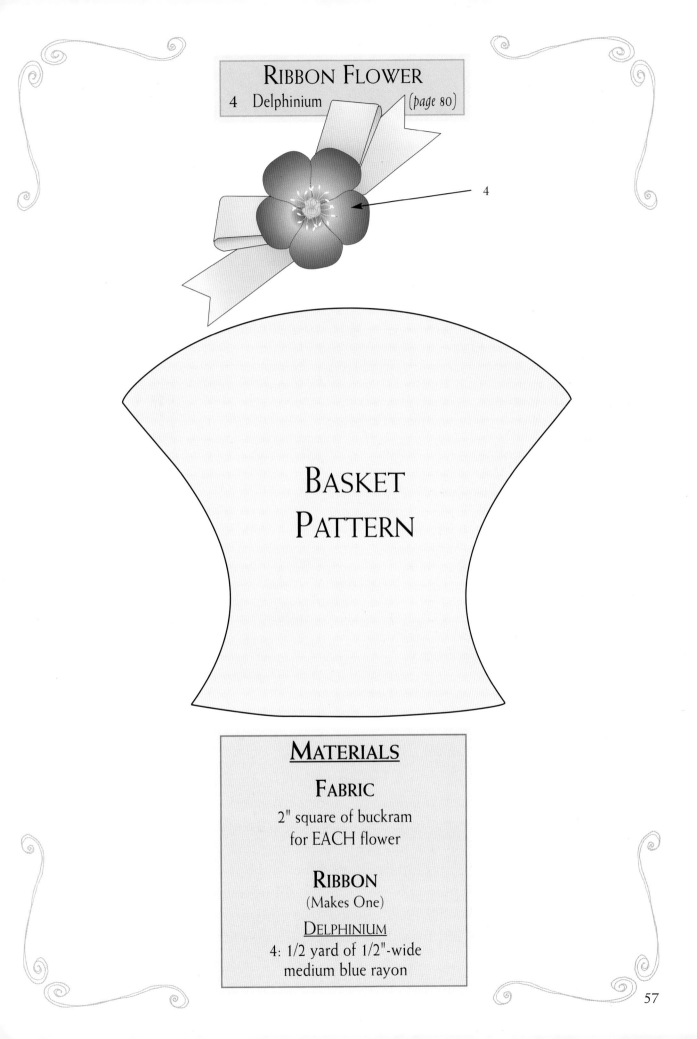

4

BASKET
PATTERN

MATERIALS

FABRIC

2" square of buckram
for EACH flower

RIBBON
(Makes One)

DELPHINIUM
4: 1/2 yard of 1/2"-wide
medium blue rayon

Padded Hanger

Trim a trio of satin padded hangers with ribbon roses and sweet peas, or create a special coverlet for the bride's dress hanger from bridal taffeta trimmed with eyelet lace. Trace the curve of the hanger shape, add the desired length of the cover, and add seam allowances. Cut the front and back from taffeta and sew them together with right sides facing, leaving a top opening for inserting the hanger. Trim and clip the seams and narrow-hem the top opening. Hem the bottom edge. Add eyelet lace trim. Make each flower individually on a square of buckram. Trim the buckram close to the stitching before attaching each flower to a cotton-wrapped floral wire stem. Add a wired pearl cluster and tie with a satin bow around the hanger hook.

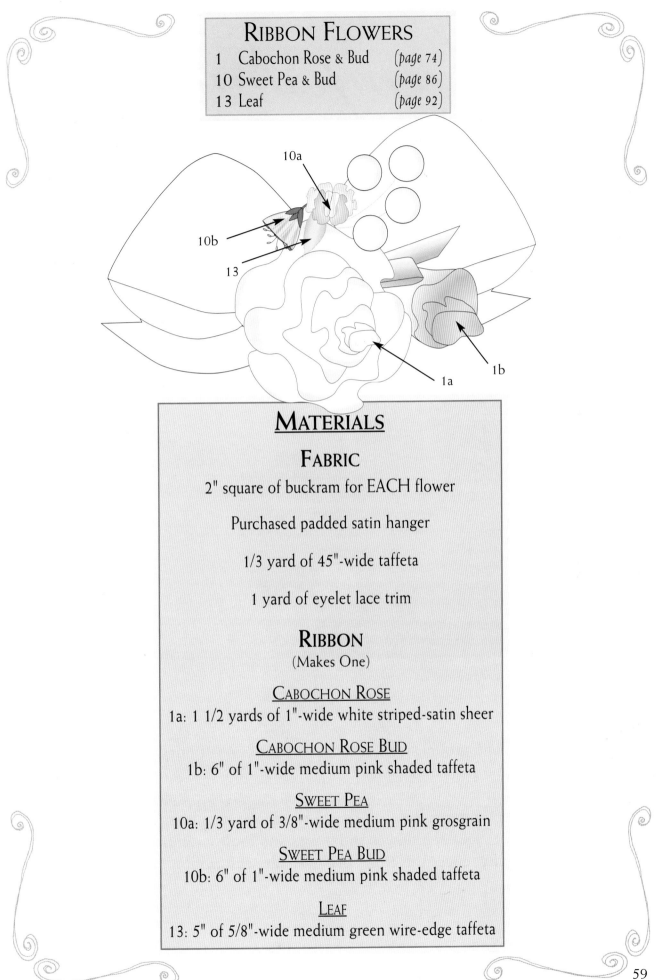

MATERIALS

FABRIC

2" square of buckram for EACH flower

Purchased padded satin hanger

1/3 yard of 45"-wide taffeta

1 yard of eyelet lace trim

RIBBON
(Makes One)

CABOCHON ROSE
1a: 1 1/2 yards of 1"-wide white striped-satin sheer

CABOCHON ROSE BUD
1b: 6" of 1"-wide medium pink shaded taffeta

SWEET PEA
10a: 1/3 yard of 3/8"-wide medium pink grosgrain

SWEET PEA BUD
10b: 6" of 1"-wide medium pink shaded taffeta

LEAF
13: 5" of 5/8"-wide medium green wire-edge taffeta

Lampshade

Bid the bride and groom sweet dreams with a ribbon-trimmed lampshade for the lamp on the nightstand. Make each flower individually on a square of buckram. (Centers of flowers can be ruched grosgrain.) Trim the buckram close to the stitching. Glue each flower to the shade, adding a 1/8"-wide ribbon streamer for each flower and leaves and loops as desired.

For finishing, cover the edges of the shade with ribbon to match the bride's colors.

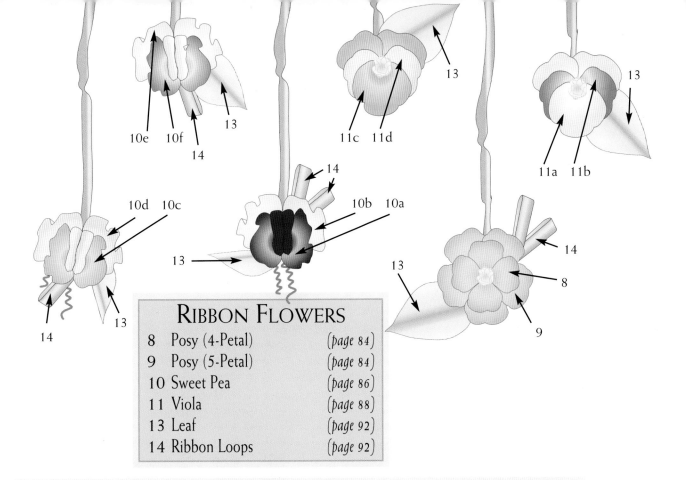

RIBBON FLOWERS

8	Posy (4-Petal)	*(page 84)*
9	Posy (5-Petal)	*(page 84)*
10	Sweet Pea	*(page 86)*
11	Viola	*(page 88)*
13	Leaf	*(page 92)*
14	Ribbon Loops	*(page 92)*

MATERIALS

FABRIC

2" square of buckram for EACH flower

Purchased lampshade and lamp

RIBBON
(Makes One)

<u>POSY (4-PETAL)</u>

8: 8" of 1/2"-wide
light blue grosgrain

<u>POSY (5-PETAL)</u>
9: 9" of 1/2"-wide
light blue grosgrain

<u>SWEET PEA</u>
10a, b, c, d, e, f: 1/3 yard of 1/2"-wide
light lavender (a)
OR dark blue (b) OR light pink (c)
OR medium pink (d)
OR light purple (e)
OR dark purple (f) grosgrain

<u>VIOLA</u>
11a, b: 1/4 yard of 1/2"-wide
light lavender (a) AND
5" of 1/2"-wide
medium lavender (b) grosgrain

11c, d: 1/4 yard of 1/2"-wide
medium pink (c) AND
5" of 1/2"-wide
light pink (d) grosgrain

<u>LEAF</u>
13: 2" of 1/2"-wide
pale green grosgrain

<u>RIBBON LOOPS</u>

14: 3" of 1/8"-wide
light green shaded rayon

THE MEMORIES

Photo Frame

Video Box Cover

Keepsake Box

Memory Wreath

Photo Frame

Memories are in the making with treasured moments from the wedding ceremony and reception framed forever! (The bride featured here chose to make a memory of dancing with her father at the wedding reception.) Purchase a moiré taffeta covered frame (ours is 7 1/2" x 9 1/2"). Glue knotted satin braid around the photo opening, if desired. Make each flower individually on a square of buckram. (Centers of flowers can be French knots or stamens.) Trim the buckram close to the stitching. Glue each flower to the frame, positioning flowers as desired.

For finishing, add purchased wired bead clusters.

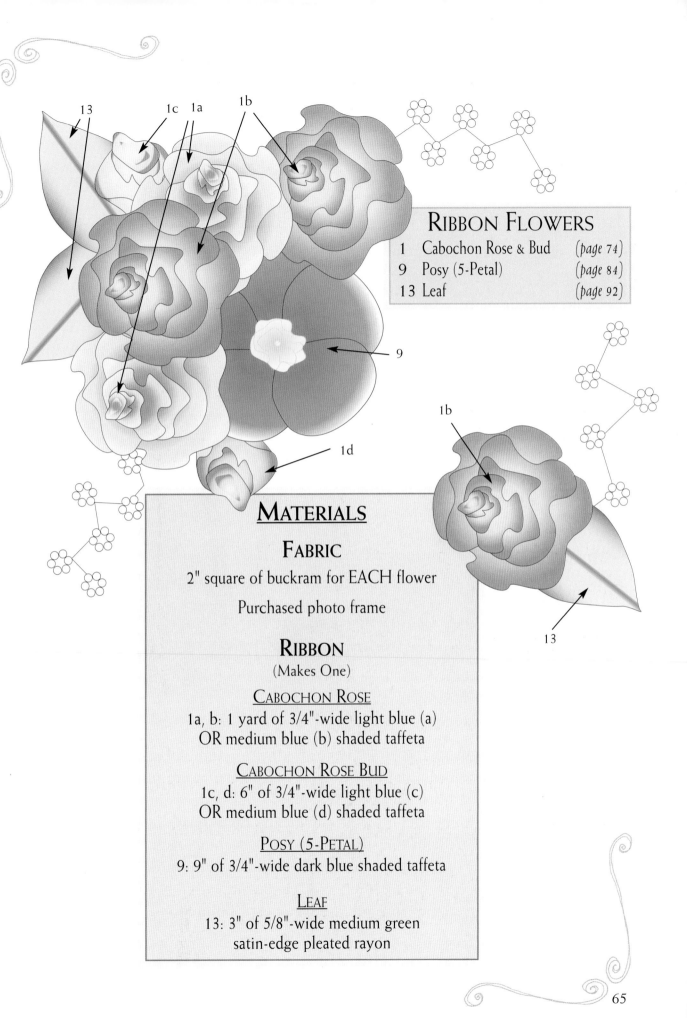

RIBBON FLOWERS

1	Cabochon Rose & Bud	*(page 74)*
9	Posy (5-Petal)	*(page 84)*
13	Leaf	*(page 92)*

MATERIALS

FABRIC

2" square of buckram for EACH flower

Purchased photo frame

RIBBON

(Makes One)

CABOCHON ROSE

1a, b: 1 yard of 3/4"-wide light blue (a)
OR medium blue (b) shaded taffeta

CABOCHON ROSE BUD

1c, d: 6" of 3/4"-wide light blue (c)
OR medium blue (d) shaded taffeta

POSY (5-PETAL)

9: 9" of 3/4"-wide dark blue shaded taffeta

LEAF

13: 3" of 5/8"-wide medium green
satin-edge pleated rayon

The newlyweds will have lasting memories of the ceremony and reception with a videotape recording of the festivities. Trim the moiré taffeta cover to coordinate with the guest book and use similar ribbon flowers and heirloom ribbon to match. Make each flower individually on a square of buckram. Trim the buckram close to the stitching before attaching each flower to the center of the 3" circle of buckram. Glue the buckram foundation to the cover of the video box (ours is 4 1/2" x 8") and trim with a border of antique ribbon. Fill in with several soft, picot-edge sheer ribbon loops and pleated leaves as desired.

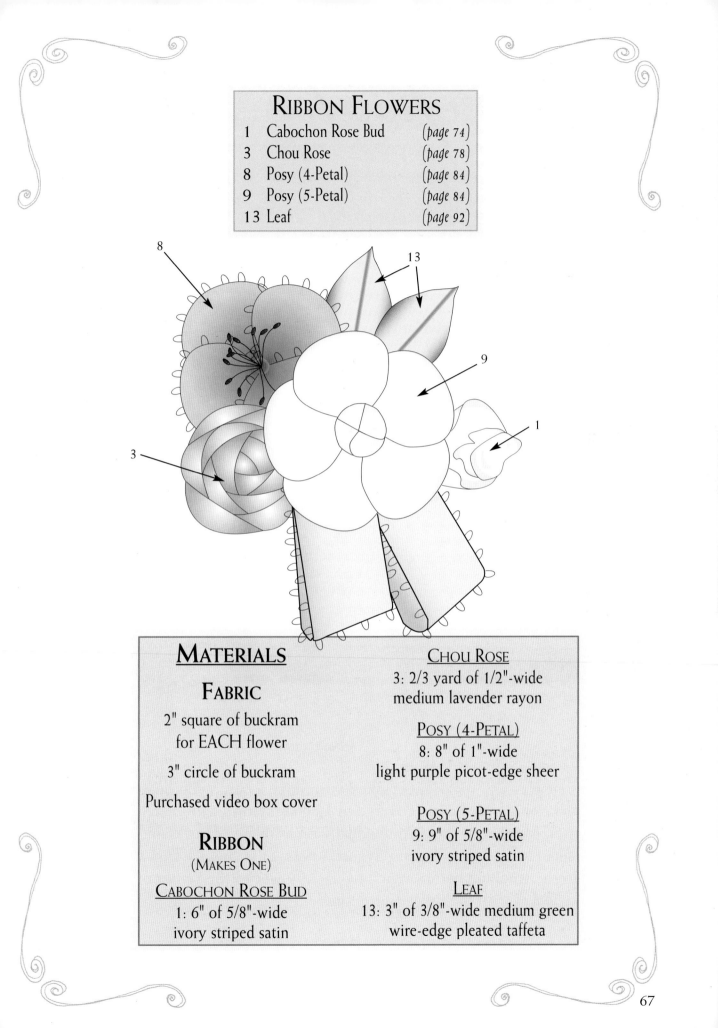

RIBBON FLOWERS

1	Cabochon Rose Bud	*(page 74)*
3	Chou Rose	*(page 78)*
8	Posy (4-Petal)	*(page 84)*
9	Posy (5-Petal)	*(page 84)*
13	Leaf	*(page 92)*

MATERIALS

FABRIC

2" square of buckram
for EACH flower

3" circle of buckram

Purchased video box cover

RIBBON
(MAKES ONE)

CABOCHON ROSE BUD
1: 6" of 5/8"-wide
ivory striped satin

CHOU ROSE
3: 2/3 yard of 1/2"-wide
medium lavender rayon

POSY (4-PETAL)
8: 8" of 1"-wide
light purple picot-edge sheer

POSY (5-PETAL)
9: 9" of 5/8"-wide
ivory striped satin

LEAF
13: 3" of 3/8"-wide medium green
wire-edge pleated taffeta

Keepsake Box

For the newlyweds' special keepsakes, customize a purchased heart-shaped box. The one shown here is covered in Jacquard fabric with matching braid and tassel. Make each flower individually on a square of buckram. (Centers of flowers can be ruched grosgrain, French knots, or stamens.) Trim the buckram close to the stitching before attaching each flower to the center of the box lid. Mix leaves with the flowers as desired.

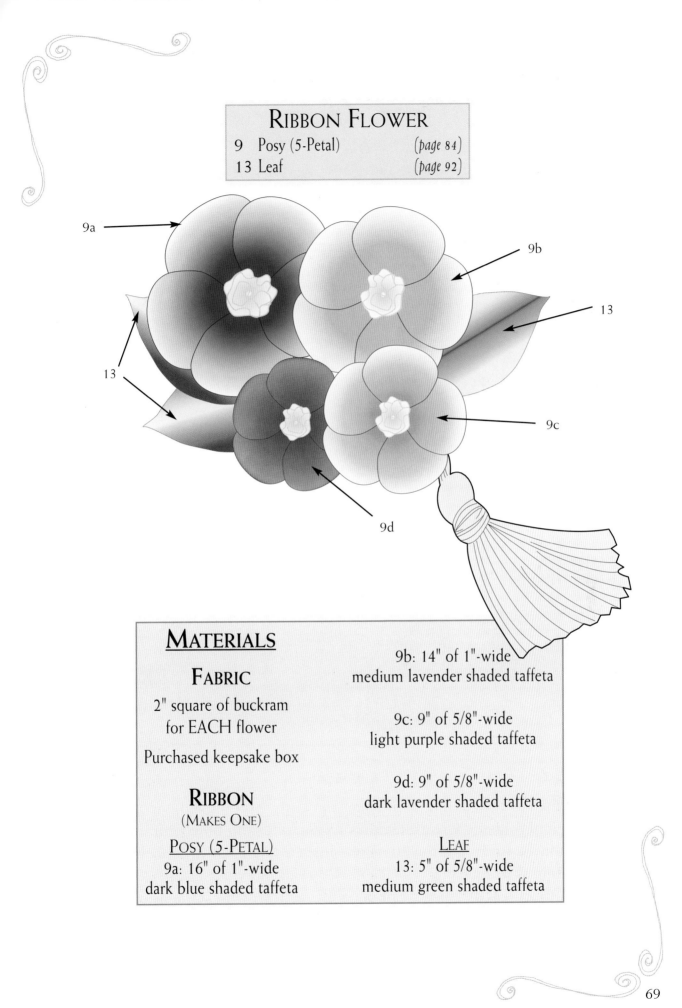

RIBBON FLOWER

| 9 | Posy (5-Petal) | (page 84) |
| 13 | Leaf | (page 92) |

9a

9b

13

13

9c

9d

MATERIALS

FABRIC

2" square of buckram
for EACH flower

Purchased keepsake box

RIBBON
(MAKES ONE)

<u>POSY (5-PETAL)</u>
9a: 16" of 1"-wide
dark blue shaded taffeta

9b: 14" of 1"-wide
medium lavender shaded taffeta

9c: 9" of 5/8"-wide
light purple shaded taffeta

9d: 9" of 5/8"-wide
dark lavender shaded taffeta

<u>LEAF</u>
13: 5" of 5/8"-wide
medium green shaded taffeta

Memory Wreath

Wreath the newlyweds' home in memories with this unique housewarming gift. The dried-flower wreath features a generous satin bow with individual flowers for the bride and the groom beneath a single white cabochon rose, symbolizing their new unity. Make each flower individually on a square of buckram. (Centers of flowers can be fabric buttons with stamens or seed beads.) Trim the buckram close to the stitching before attaching a flower to each of the satin ribbon tails.

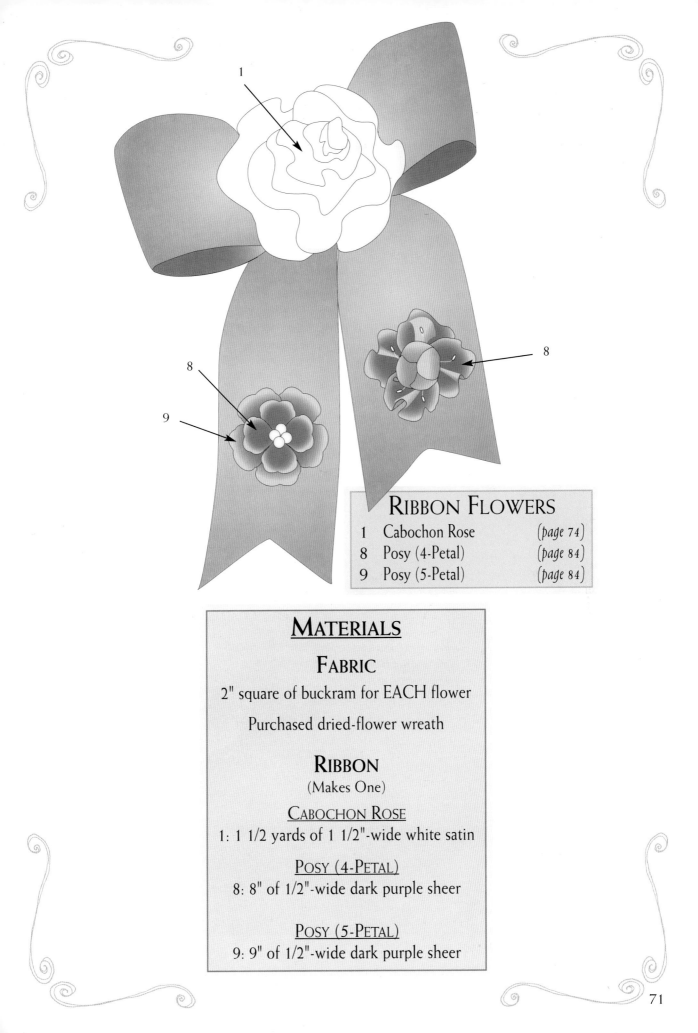

RIBBON FLOWERS

1	Cabochon Rose	*(page 74)*
8	Posy (4-Petal)	*(page 84)*
9	Posy (5-Petal)	*(page 84)*

MATERIALS

FABRIC

2" square of buckram for EACH flower

Purchased dried-flower wreath

RIBBON
(Makes One)

CABOCHON ROSE
1: 1 1/2 yards of 1 1/2"-wide white satin

POSY (4-PETAL)
8: 8" of 1/2"-wide dark purple sheer

POSY (5-PETAL)
9: 9" of 1/2"-wide dark purple sheer

THE RIBBON FLOWERS

Cabochon Rose & Bud

Camellia

Chou Rose

Delphinium

Fan Flower

Heather Rose

Posy

Sweet Pea & Bud

Viola

Wedding Rose

Leaf

Ribbon Loops

M Bow

Cabochon Rose & Bud

1. To make a bud, fold down about 2" on the right-hand end of the ribbon as shown so that 1" hangs below to form a "handle." **2.** Fold the outermost half of the handle over onto the other half. This will become the center of the rose. **3.** Now roll the handle from right to left, coiling the ribbon loosely to make the rolled center of the rose.
4. When you have coiled two or three turns, and the top is a perfect circle, fold the top selvage back to form a gentle bias fold, which will become the edge of a rose petal. Roll the rose to the left, so that the bias fold becomes part of the center. Hold the "handle" in your right hand as you roll; this will keep the rose loosely rolled. Secure the ribbon at the base of the rose with a few stitches. Repeat this rolling and folding step once more, stitching to secure. **5.** Sew the center bud through the lower selvage onto the buckram.
6. To make a rose, repeat steps 1–5, then stitch along the lower selvage of the ribbon and gather it loosely. Securing the gathered ribbon from underneath, gently wind it around the center bud in the same direction as you rolled the center, allowing a 1/4" space between the gathered rows until it resembles a full-blown rose. When it is firmly attached to the buckram, trim the buckram close to the stitching.

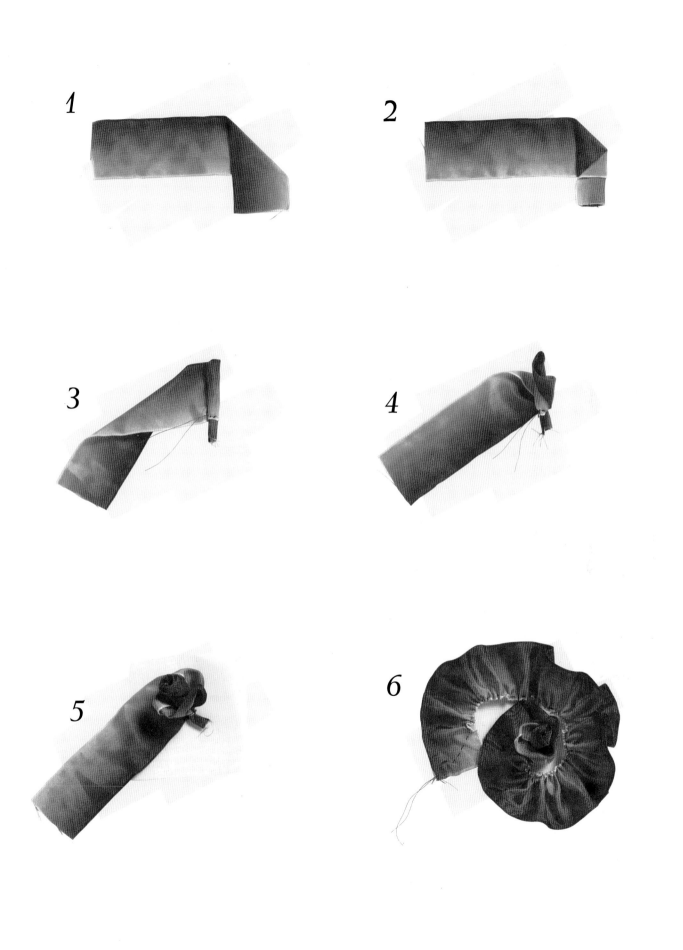

Camellia

1. Cut six 6" pieces of ribbon for the lower petals. Starting on the upper edge 1/8" from one end, take a few stitches vertically to the lower edge. Sew gathering stitches along the lower edge of the ribbon; then take a few stitches vertically to the upper edge. **2.** Pull the thread tight and knot it. Repeat to make six petals. **3.** Join the petals with running stitches on the gathered edge, overlapping each petal. **4.** Pull the thread tight to close the center of the flower; knot and clip the thread. Sew the flower to the buckram square. **5.** Cut three 5" pieces of ribbon for the middle petals. Starting on the upper edge 1/8" from one end, take a few stitches vertically to the lower edge. Sew gathering stitches along the lower edge of the ribbon; then take a few stitches vertically to the upper edge. **6.** Pull the thread tight and knot it. Repeat to make three petals. **7.** Join the petals with running stitches on the gathered edge, overlapping each petal. Pull the thread tight to close the center of the flower; knot and clip the thread. **8.** Sew the flower to the lower petals.

1

2

3

4

5

6

7

8

Chou Rose

1. Cut a 2"-diameter circle from the buckram and carefully slash it from the edge to the center. Overlap the cut edges about 1" and stitch them together along the edge, forming a cone shape. **2.** Turn under 1/4" at one end of the ribbon and place over the top of the cone. Using a knotted double thread, secure the ribbon to the buckram along the folded end and along the side edges with small running stitches. Let the needle and thread dangle in readiness for the next stitches. **3.** Swing the ribbon counterclockwise a quarter turn, creating a diagonal fold on top of the cone. Stitch across the width of the ribbon from the lower right corner to the upper corner. **4.** Swing the ribbon counterclockwise another quarter turn, again creating a diagonal fold on top of the cone. Stitch across the width of the ribbon from the upper right corner to the upper left corner. **5.** Make a third quarter turn and stitch across the width again, gradually curving your line of stitches to follow the natural curve of the cone. **6.** Make another quarter turn and secure the ribbon across the width to the buckram. A small "window" should become visible in the center of the cone. **7.** Position your subsequent folds just enough below the previous folds so the folds are not covered up—they form the petals of the rose. **8.** When the cone is completely covered with folds, trim the remaining length of ribbon and secure the end to the back of the buckram. If you are using a short ribbon that does not cover the whole cone, trim the exposed buckram and secure the end of the ribbon to the back.

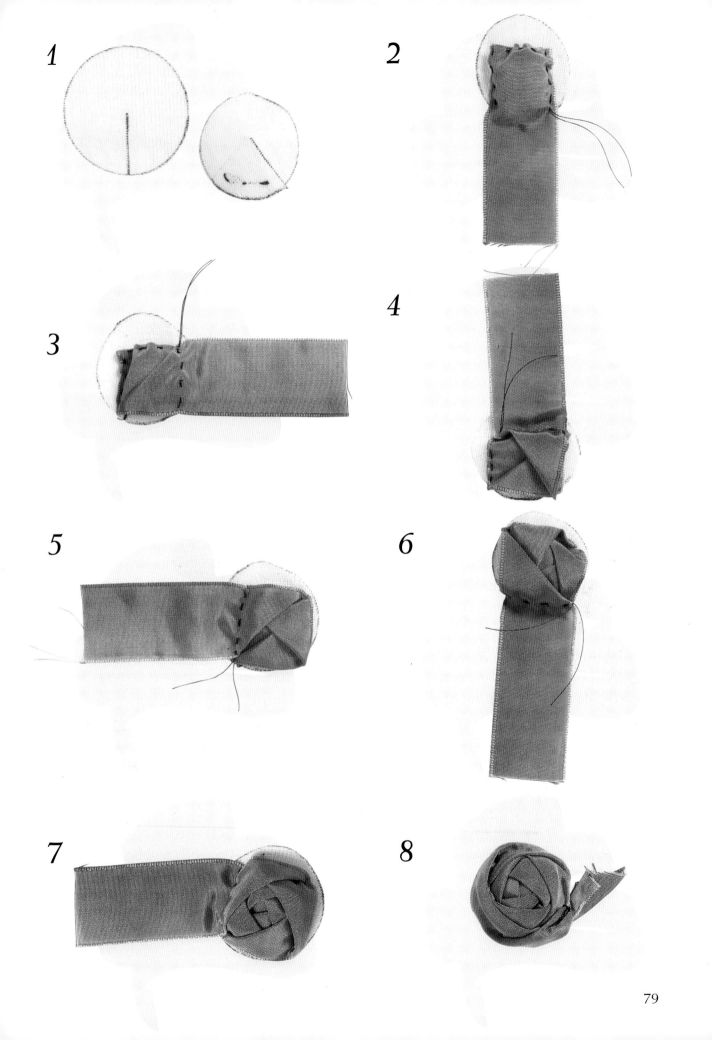

Delphinium

1. Cut one 7 3/4" piece of ribbon. Divide it into five equal intervals. Starting on the top edge, 1/8" from one end and using double thread, take about three stitches vertically to the bottom edge. Sew along the bottom edge to nearly the end of the interval. Next take about three stitches to the next mark on the top edge. Sew along the top edge to nearly the end of the interval. Repeat to the end. **2.** Pull the thread tight. **3.** Join the first petal to the last petal, rotating each petal outward at the vertical stitching. Knot the thread and sew the flower to the buckram. **4.** Cut one 5 1/4" piece of ribbon. Divide it into three equal intervals. Stitch as in step 1. **5.** Pull the thread tight. Join the first petal to the last petal, rotating each petal outward at the vertical stitching. **6.** Knot the thread and sew the flower to the first petals.

Fan Flower

1. Cut one 4" piece of ribbon. Stitch through the bottom edge of the pleats. **2.** Pull the thread tight. **3.** Knot the thread. **4.** Add stamens to the center if desired. Join the ends of the flower. Stitch the seam. Turn the flower right side out.

Heather Rose

1. Cut one 20" piece of ribbon. Divide it into six equal intervals. Starting at the beginning of the first interval and using double thread take three or four stitches vertically to the opposite edge. Sew along the opposite edge to the end of the interval. Pull the thread tight. **2.** Repeat for the remaining intervals. **3.** Rotate each petal outward at the vertical stitching. Knot the thread. Join the first petal to the last petal. Sew the flower to the buckram. **4.** Cut one 17" piece of ribbon. Divide it into five equal intervals. Starting at the first interval from one end and using double thread take three or four stitches vertically to the opposite edge. Sew along the opposite edge. Pull the thread tight. Repeat for the remaining intervals. **5.** Rotate each petal outward at the vertical stitching. Knot the thread. Join the first petal to the last petal. Sew the flower to the first layer of petals. **6.** For the center, cut one 8 1/2" piece of ribbon. Fold forward about 3 1/4" on the left-hand end of the ribbon to form a triangle. **7.** At the top corner, leave about 1/8" space so the selvages from both the left and the right sides of the ribbon almost meet. Twist the ribbon backward to form a second triangle. **8.** At the second corner, leave about 1/8" space so the selvages from both the left and the right sides of the ribbon almost meet. Twist the ribbon backward to form a third triangle and complete the square. **9.** Stitch around the outer edges of the square. **10.** Pull up the thread to form a loose or tight button center. Secure the button to the center of the flower.

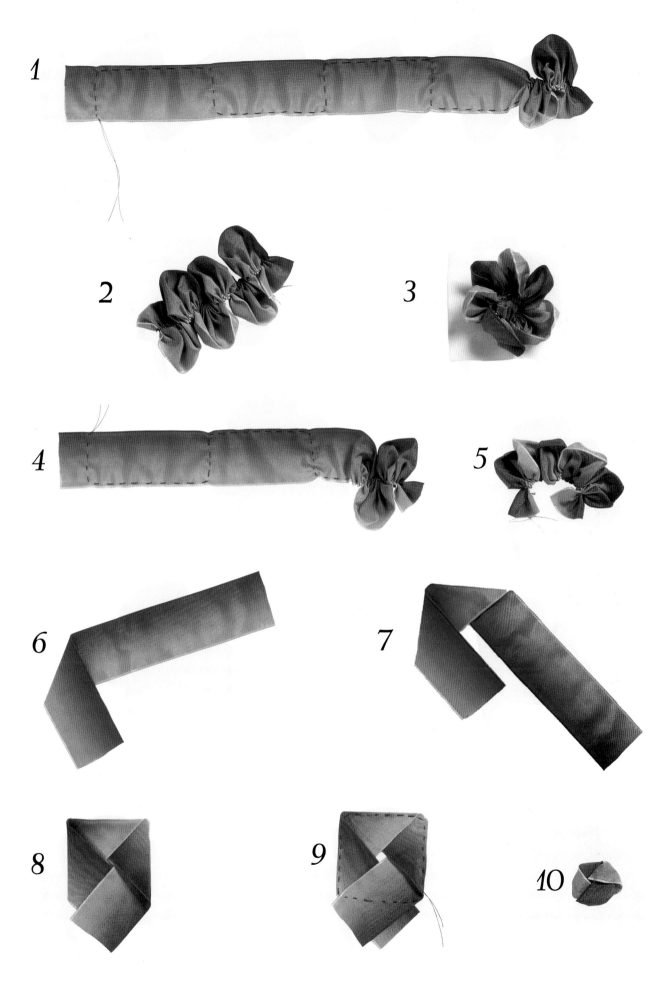

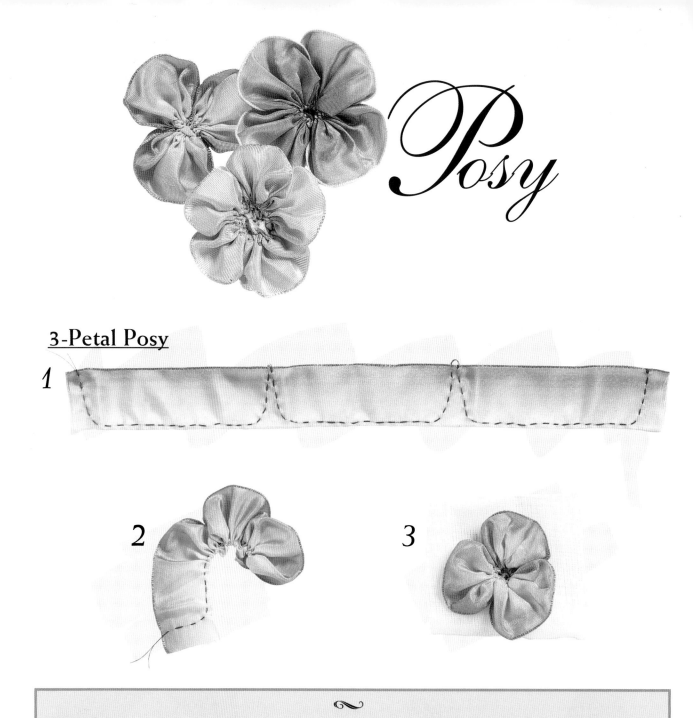

Posy

3-Petal Posy

1. Divide the ribbon into three equal intervals. Starting on the top edge, 1/8" from one end and using double thread, sew a few running stitches diagonally to the bottom edge. Sew along the bottom edge to almost the end of the interval. Next stitch upward diagonally to the interval mark on the top edge. Carry a stitch over the top edge and stitch diagonally to the bottom edge. Repeat to the end. **2.** Pull the thread to gather the ribbon. Join the first petal to the last petal, then pull the thread tighter. Knot the thread and sew the flower to the buckram. **3.** Trim the buckram close to the stitching in back.

4-Petal Posy

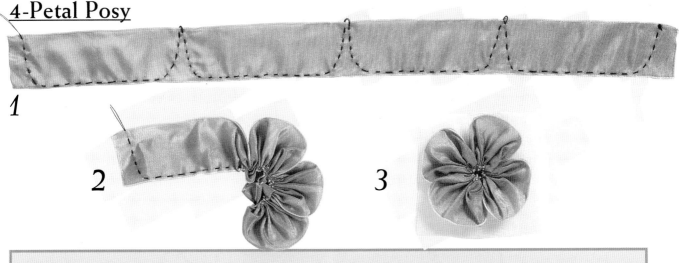

1. Divide the ribbon into four equal intervals. Starting on the top edge, 1/8" from one end and using double thread, sew a few running stitches diagonally to the bottom edge. Sew along the bottom edge to almost the end of the interval. Next stitch upward diagonally to the interval mark on the top edge. Carry a stitch over the top edge and stitch diagonally to the bottom edge. Repeat to the end. **2.** Pull the thread to gather the ribbon. Join the first petal to the last petal, then pull the thread tighter. Knot the thread and sew the flower to the buckram. **3.** Trim the buckram close to the stitching in back.

5-Petal Posy

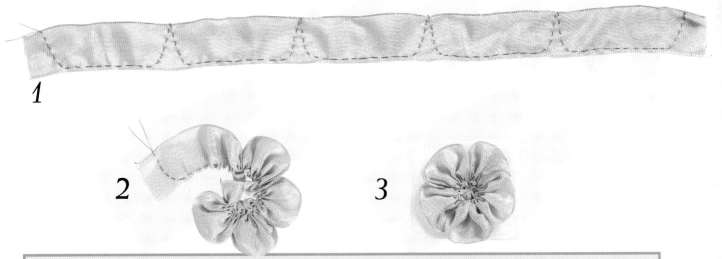

1. Divide the ribbon into five equal intervals. Starting on the top edge, 1/8" from one end and using double thread, sew a few running stitches diagonally to the bottom edge. Sew along the bottom edge to almost the end of the interval. Next stitch upward diagonally to the interval mark on the top edge. Carry a stitch over the top edge and stitch diagonally to the bottom edge. Repeat to the end. **2.** Pull the thread to gather the ribbon. Join the first petal to the last petal, then pull the thread tighter. Knot the thread and sew the flower to the buckram. **3.** Trim the buckram close to the stitching in back.

Sweet Pea & Bud

1. Cut one piece of ribbon as specified in the cutting chart. Divide the ribbon into two even intervals. Starting on the top edge, 1/8" from one end and using double thread, take a few stitches diagonally to the bottom edge. Sew along the bottom edge to almost the end of the interval. Next stitch upward diagonally to the interval mark on the top edge. Carry a stitch over the top edge and stitch diagonally to the bottom edge. Sew along the bottom edge to almost the end of the interval. Take a few stitches to the top edge. **2.** Pull the thread tight and knot it. **3.** Sew the petals to the buckram. **4.** Repeat step 1. **5.** Repeat step 2. **6.** Repeat step 3, layering the petals onto the buckram. **7.** For the center, cut one piece of ribbon as specified in the cutting chart and fold it in half. Stitch along the bottom edge. **8.** Pull the thread tight. **9.** Knot the thread. Layer it on the buckram in the center of the layered petals to complete the flower. Trim the buckram close to the stitching in back. **10.** For the bud, repeat the stitching in step 1 using the ribbon specified in the project materials list. **11.** Repeat step 2. Add stamens. Secure with cotton-wrapped floral wire. **12.** Fold the petals together.

Ribbon Length	Step 1	Step 4	Step 7
1/3 yard	Cut one 4 1/2" piece	Cut one 4 1/2" piece	Cut one 2" piece
3/4 yard	Cut one 10 1/2" piece	Cut one 10 1/2" piece	Cut one 5" piece

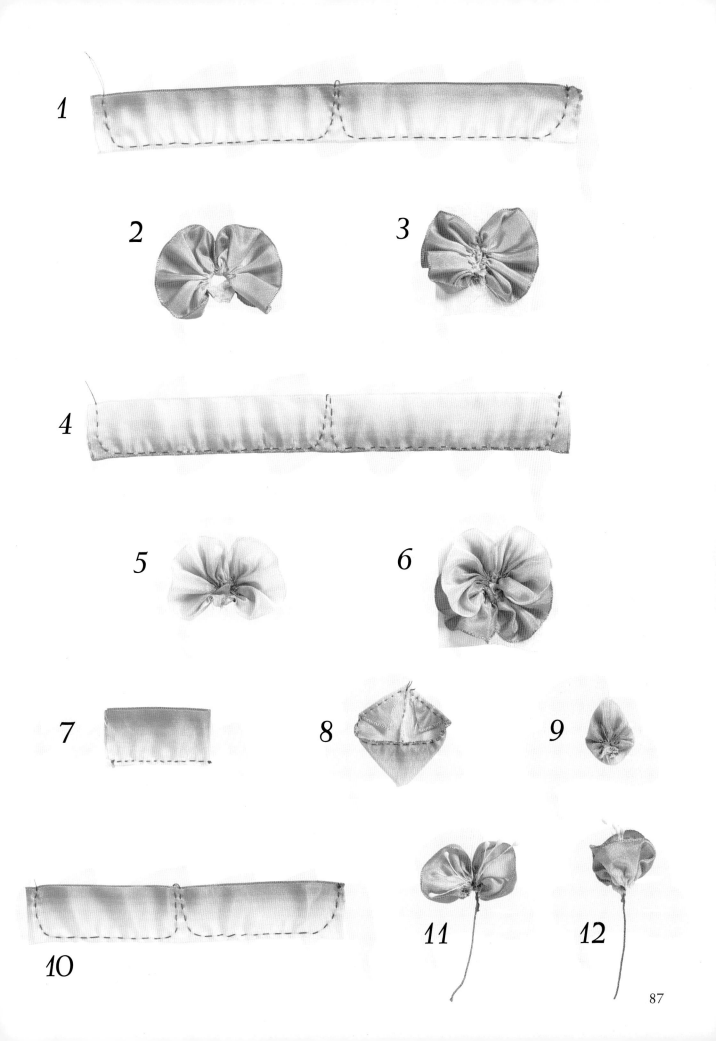

1

2

3

4

5

6

7

8

9

10

11

12

Viola

1. Cut a 5" piece of ribbon. (If you are using two colors of ribbon, as in the dress trims or celebration flutes, cut 5" from the longer ribbon.) Divide the ribbon into two equal intervals. Starting on the top edge, 1/8" from one end and using double thread, take a few stitches diagonally to the bottom edge. Sew along the bottom edge to almost the end of the interval. Next stitch upward diagonally to the interval mark on the top edge. Carry a stitch over the top edge and stitch diagonally to the bottom edge. Sew along the bottom edge to almost the end of the interval. Take a few stitches to the top edge. **2.** Pull the thread tight to gather the ribbon. Backstitch and knot the thread. **3.** Sew the gathers to the top half of the buckram square. **4.** Cut a 4 1/2" piece of ribbon. (If you are using two colors, cut 4 1/2" from the shorter ribbon.) Repeat step 1 with this piece of ribbon. **5.** Repeat step 2. **6.** Sew the gathers to the buckram square slightly below the first gathers. **7.** Cut a 2 1/2" piece of ribbon. (If you are using two colors, use the same color you used in step 1.) Beginning on the bottom edge, 1/8" from one end and using a double thread, sew a few stitches diagonally to the top edge. **8.** Pull the thread tight to gather the ribbon. Backstitch and knot the thread. **9.** Sew the gathered ribbon to the top gathers of ribbon, stitching through the buckram at the same time. Trim the buckram close to the stitching in back.

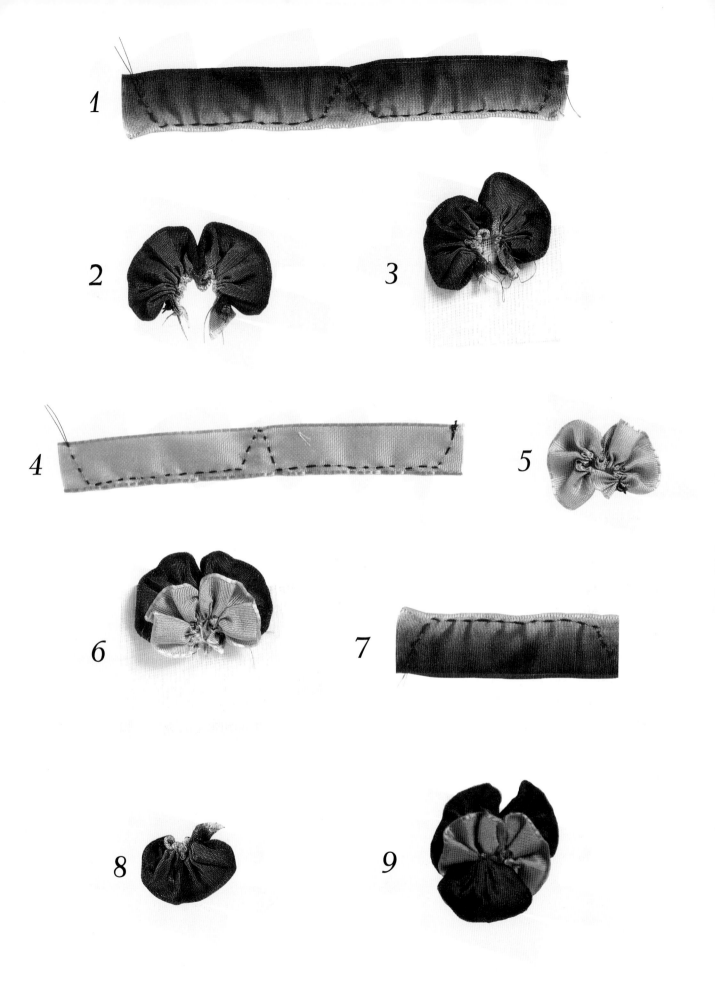

Wedding Rose

1. Cut a 28" piece of ribbon. Divide the ribbon into six equal intervals. Starting 1/8" from one end and using double thread take three or four stitches vertically to the opposite edge. Sew along the opposite edge to the end of the interval. Take three or four stitches vertically. Sew along the opposite edge to the end of the interval. Repeat to the end. Pull the thread tight. **2.** Rotate each petal outward at the vertical stitching. Knot the thread. **3.** Join the first petal to the last petal. Sew the flower to the buckram. **4.** Cut a 6" piece of ribbon. Make a bud in the style of a cabochon rose bud (see page 74). Sew the bud to the buckram at the center of the flower. Trim the buckram close to the stitching in back.

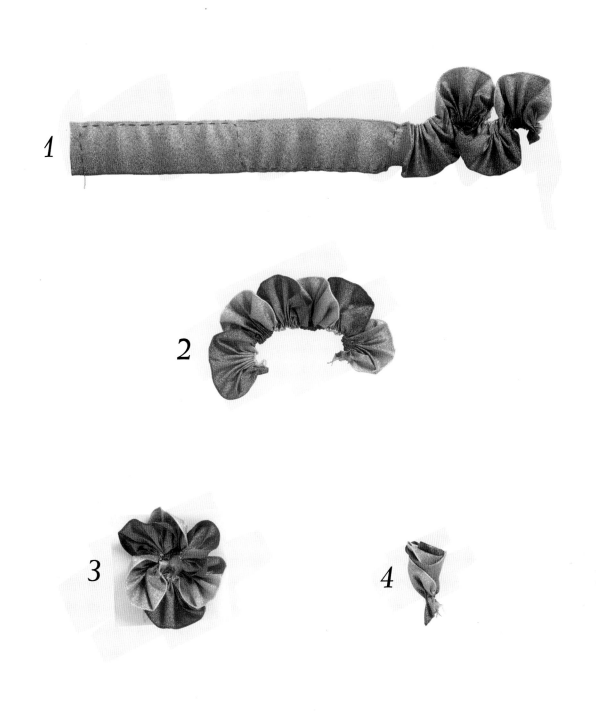

Leaf

1 **2**

1. Fold the ribbon in half widthwise, then turn up the left corner. Trim the right corner at an angle. With double thread, sew a small running stitch down the diagonal cut edge, along the bottom edge, and up the opposite diagonal edge. **2.** Pull up the thread slightly, but do not knot it. Open the layers and arrange the gathers carefully, keeping most of them in the center and toward the bottom of the leaf. Secure the thread with three to four stitches in the seam.

Ribbon Loops

1. Cut a 3" piece of ribbon for each loop. **2.** Fold ribbon in half lengthwise, and sew the ends to the buckram. **3.** Repeat to make as many loops as desired.

M Bow

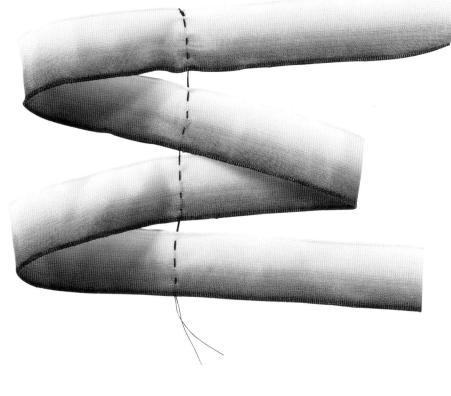

1. Arrange a length of ribbon in an M shape. Using short running stitches, sew through the center of each of the four legs. **2.** Gently pull up the gathering threads, forming a nice, soft bow.

ACKNOWLEDGEMENTS

I would like to thank all of the members of my
family, especially my husband, Steve, for
their continuing support.

Many thanks once again
to my staff members at The Ribbonry
for all their hard work:
Alice Croy,
Marguerite Nagy,
Jan Niles,
Natalie Tallon,
Marge Tiefenbach,
Alice Parsons,
and Gloria Weller.

Thank you also to Roger Zielinski
for the use of his beautiful rose garden,
and for his creativity and artistry
in the delphinium arches and all floral arrangements;
chef Audrey Chabot for her exquisite catering;
Patty Auman, for her designer bridal fashions;
and Laura Berkowitz;
Hazel Hayden;
Dana and Taylor Hess;
Claire, Emily, and Susan Oulette;
and Roseanne Nitschke.

Camela

SOURCES & SUPPLIES

To make the ribbon flowers and projects, you'll need the following: general sewing supplies, tacky fabric glue, buckram, felt, purchased stamens, wired pearl clusters and seed beads, cotton-wrapped floral wire, soutache braid, pin backs.

For the seating bows shown on page 38, the heart-shaped wire basket filled with moss and dried flowers is called a Heart Swing and is available from Calyx & Corolla, The Flower Lover's Flower Company (888/88-CALYX).

For the satin-covered oval, square, and heart-shaped boxes with tasseled lids shown throughout, special arrangements have been made with Carr's Country Florist and Gift in Brandon, VT, to make them available by mail order (802/247-5727).

For all other specialty ribbon supplies including imported ribbons, wired ribbons, Hymen Hendler ribbons, Mokuba ribbons, books, videos, kits, buckram, and stamens call (or visit!) Camela Nitschke's shop, The Ribbonry, 119 Louisiana Ave., Perrysburg, OH 43551 (419/872-0073), www.ribbonry.com. Retail, wholesale, and mail-order options are available.

Books from Martingale & Company

Crafts
15 Beads
The Art of Handmade Paper and Collage
Christmas Ribbonry
Fabric Mosaics
Folded Fabric Fun
Hand-Stitched Samplers from I Done My Best
The Home Decorator's Stamping Book
Making Memories
A Passion for Ribbonry
Stamp with Style

Home Decorating
Decorate with Quilts & Collections
The Home Decorator's Stamping Book
Living with Little Quilts
Make Room for Quilts
Special-Occasion Table Runners
Stitch & Stencil
Welcome Home: Debbie Mumm
Welcome Home: Kaffe Fassett

Knitting
Simply Beautiful Sweaters
Two Sticks and a String
Welcome Home: Kaffe Fassett

Stitchery/Needle Arts
Christmas Ribbonry
Crazy Rags
Hand-Stitched Samplers from I Done My Best
Machine Needlelace
Miniature Baltimore Album Quilts
A Passion for Ribbonry
A Silk-Ribbon Album
Victorian Elegance

Surface Design/Fabric Manipulation
15 Beads
Complex Cloth
Creative Marbling on Fabric
Dyes & Paints
Hand-Dyed Fabric Made Easy
Jazz It Up

Wearables
Crazy Rags
Dress Daze
Easy Reversible Vests
Jacket Jazz Encore
Just Like Mommy
Variations in Chenille

Quilts

Appliqué
Appliqué in Bloom
Baltimore Bouquets
Basic Quiltmaking Techniques for Hand Appliqué
Basic Quiltmaking Techniques for Machine Appliqué
Coxcomb Quilt
The Easy Art of Appliqué
Folk Art Animals
From a Quilter's Garden
Fun with Sunbonnet Sue
Garden Appliqué
Interlacing Borders
Once Upon a Quilt
Stars in the Garden
Sunbonnet Sue All Through the Year
Welcome to the North Pole

Basic Quiltmaking Techniques
Basic Quiltmaking Techniques for Borders & Bindings
Basic Quiltmaking Techniques for Curved Piecing
Basic Quiltmaking Techniques for Divided Circles
Basic Quiltmaking Techniques for Eight-Pointed Stars
Basic Quiltmaking Techniques for Hand Appliqué

Basic Quiltmaking Techniques for Machine Appliqué
Basic Quiltmaking Techniques for Strip Piecing
Your First Quilt Book (or it should be!)

Design Reference
Color: The Quilter's Guide
Design Essentials: The Quilter's Guide
Design Your Own Quilts
The Nature of Design
QuiltSkills

Foundation/Paper Piecing
Classic Quilts with Precise Foundation Piecing
Crazy but Pieceable
Easy Machine Paper Piecing
Easy Mix & Match Machine Paper Piecing
Easy Paper-Pieced Keepsake Quilts
Easy Paper-Pieced Miniatures
Easy Reversible Vests
Go Wild with Quilts
Go Wild with Quilts—Again!
It's Raining Cats & Dogs
Mariner's Medallion
Paper Piecing the Seasons
A Quilter's Ark
Sewing on the Line
Show Me How to Paper Piece

Joy of Quilting Series
Borders by Design
The Easy Art of Appliqué
A Fine Finish
Hand-Dyed Fabric Made Easy
Happy Endings
Loving Stitches
Machine Quilting Made Easy
A Perfect Match
Press for Success
Sensational Settings
Shortcuts
The Ultimate Book of Quilt Labels

Machine Quilting/Sewing
Machine Needlelace
Machine Quilting Made Easy
Machine Quilting with Decorative Threads
Quilting Makes the Quilt
Thread Magic
Threadplay

Miniature/Small Quilts
Celebrate! with Little Quilts
Crazy but Pieceable
Easy Paper-Pieced Miniatures
Fun with Miniature Log Cabin Blocks
Little Quilts All Through the House
Living with Little Quilts
Miniature Baltimore Album Quilts
Small Quilts Made Easy
Small Wonders

Quilting/Finishing Techniques
Borders by Design
The Border Workbook
A Fine Finish
Happy Endings
Interlacing Borders
Loving Stitches
Quilt It!
Quilting Design Sourcebook
Quilting Makes the Quilt
Traditional Quilts with Painless Borders
The Ultimate Book of Quilt Labels

Rotary Cutting/Speed Piecing
101 Fabulous Rotary-Cut Quilts
All-Star Sampler
Around the Block with Judy Hopkins
Bargello Quilts

Basic Quiltmaking Techniques for Strip Piecing
Block by Block
Easy Seasonal Wall Quilts
Easy Star Sampler
Fat Quarter Quilts
The Heirloom Quilt
The Joy of Quilting
More Quilts for Baby
More Strip-Pieced Watercolor Magic
A New Slant on Bargello Quilts
A New Twist on Triangles
Patchwork Pantry
Quilters on the Go
Quilting Up a Storm
Quilts for Baby
Quilts from Aunt Amy
ScrapMania
Simply Scrappy Quilts
Square Dance
Strip-Pieced Watercolor Magic
Stripples Strikes Again!
Strips That Sizzle
Two-Color Quilts

Seasonal Projects
Christmas Ribbonry
Easy Seasonal Wall Quilts
Folded Fabric Fun
Holiday Happenings
Quilted for Christmas
Quilted for Christmas, Book III
Quilted for Christmas, Book IV
A Silk-Ribbon Album
Welcome to the North Pole

Theme Quilts
The Cat's Meow
Everyday Angels in Extraordinary Quilts
Fabric Collage Quilts
Fabric Mosaics
Folded Fabric Fun
Folk Art Quilts
Honoring the Seasons
It's Raining Cats and Dogs
Life in the Country with Country Threads
Making Memories
More Quilts for Baby
The Nursery Rhyme Quilt
Once Upon a Quilt
Patchwork Pantry
Quilted Landscapes
Quilting Your Memories
Quilts for Baby
Quilts from Nature
Through the Window and Beyond
Two-Color Quilts

Watercolor Quilts
More Strip-Pieced Watercolor Magic
Strip-Pieced Watercolor Magic
Watercolor Impressions
Watercolor Quilts

Many of these books are available through your local quilt, fabric, craft-supply, or art-supply store. For more information, call, write, fax, or e-mail for our free full-color catalog.

Martingale & Company
PO Box 118
Bothell, WA 98041-0118 USA

1-800-426-3126
International: 1-425-483-3313
24-Hour Fax: 1-425-486-7596
Web site: www.patchwork.com
E-mail: info@martingale-pub.com

3/9